The gift of the Goddess is in your hands . . .

You can gain Goddess power by being aware of the sacred in the everyday. This sense of the sacred comes about when you notice and take time to experience the small treasures of life—moments, acts and encounters that you might otherwise overlook through hasty, unconscious behavior. As you cultivate your awareness in this way, your life may seem to expand. With this new focus, an encounter is no longer a coincidental occurrence, it is an introduction to a new facet of yourself. And when that awareness deep inside you dawns and you are able to see more, understand more and expect more from the quality of your own life, something magical happens. You start to become free—free to be who you are uniquely.

Books by Robin MacNaughton

Power Astrology
How to Seduce Any Man in the Zodiac
Goddess Power

Published by POCKET BOOKS

For orders other than by individual consumers, Pocket Books
grants a discount on the purchase of **10 or more** copies of
single titles for special markets or premium use. For further
details, please write to the Vice-President of Special Markets,
Pocket Books, 1633 Broadway, New York, NY 10019-6785,
8th Floor.

For information on how individual consumers can place
orders, please write to Mail Order Department, Simon &
Schuster Inc., 200 Old Tappan Road, Old Tappan, NJ 07675.

GODDESS POWER

AN ASTROLOGICAL GUIDE TO LIVING SACREDLY

ROBIN MACNAUGHTON

POCKET BOOKS
New York   London   Toronto   Sydney   Tokyo   Singapore

An *Original* Publication of POCKET BOOKS

POCKET BOOKS, a division of Simon & Schuster Inc.
1230 Avenue of the Americas, New York, NY 10020

ISBN: 0-671-88181-7

First Pocket Books printing December 1996

10 9 8 7 6 5 4 3 2 1

POCKET and colophon are registered trademarks of
Simon & Schuster Inc.

Cover art by Roxana Villa

Printed in the U.S.A.

This book is dedicated to all women, everywhere.

CONTENTS

Contents

PREFACE

THIS BOOK IS NOT MERELY A SPIRITUAL BOOK. IT IS also a psychological book. It is about power and feminine psychology. Therefore, it deals with some of the psychological traits and behaviors that sabotage women and rob them of their power. Singing and dancing in a circle on a Sunday afternoon may feel wonderful and give you an instant boost of self-love and confidence you need, but you still have to deal with yourself on Monday morning at work or Monday night in a marital dispute. There can be no real feminine power when you are not fully conscious of what you are really doing. Therefore, I deal with the dark as well as the light sides of consciousness. I deal with the negative as well as the potentially wonderful because that is the truth of all of us.

GODDESS
POWER

particular monster. As you cultivate your awareness in this way, your life may seem to expand. With
this new focus, an encounter is no longer a confusion

INTRODUCTION

A NEW FEMINISM IS EMERGING THAT IS SPIRITUAL. IT IS loosely referred to as the Goddess. The Goddess is embodied in acts of honoring, celebrating and living in a conscious way through the feminine principle. The feminine principle is associated with wisdom, intuition, unity, love, joy, nature and creativity in all its realms. The spirituality of the Goddess is born out of respect for nature and life in all its forms, compassion, connection with others and ourselves. It is the healing of the alienation and addiction so prevalent in the 90s.

You can gain Goddess power by being aware of the sacred in the everyday. This sense of the sacred comes about when you notice and take time to experience the small treasures of life—moments, acts and encounters that you might otherwise overlook through hasty, unconscious behavior. As you cultivate your awareness in this way, your life may seem to expand. With this new focus, an encounter is no longer a coincidental occurrence, it is an introduction to a new facet of yourself. And when that awareness deep inside you dawns and you are able to see more, understand more and expect more from the quality of your own life, something magical happens. You start to become free—free to be who you are uniquely.

Women have power. A great deal of power. However, so many women don't even know it exists or how to tap into it. The power I'm referring to is not power over something or someone. It is power from within. Power from within begins with intuition, perception, insight and understanding. It extends to compassion, love, creativity, wisdom and deep connection with others, oneself and the divine.

In ancient times, before the birth of Christ, the religion of the Goddess prevailed. Creative and all-powerful, the Goddess was the emblem of life. Life itself, the earth and the ability to create life were sacred. Rituals, referred to as Divine Mysteries, were widely practiced and involved the symbolic depiction of the cycles and transformations of life and death. Instead of the sorrowful sense of endings that seems to pervade our world today, there was the involvement and respect for life as a series of cycles that mirrored the waxing and waning cycles of the moon. After the dark phase of a cycle, there was a young new phase, a rebirth. The connections between death and life were highlighted, giving life a sense of mystery and linking death to the divine. Within Catal Huyuk, the earliest known Goddess culture, religious practice was part of everyday life. Shrines were built next to dwellings. Priestesses and families shared communal spaces and common tasks. Joy and celebration was the daily mood: The sacred was celebrated consciously in the everyday.

Today there is an extraordinary prevalence of addiction in our culture which is people's defense against the sense of deadness and emptiness in the everyday. People are disconnected spiritually because they sense that male values—competitive, cool, first, fast and nonfeeling attitudes—have been rewarded with power. As we enter the New Age, we are slowly becoming aware that those masculine values are no longer making us happy, secure, serene, nourished or vital. This is because in a predominently male culture the emphasis is placed on what's external, leaving the internal world neglected and viewed as a meaningless void. The power of the Goddess is the power of the sacred within as it extends outward and lights up all things: people, places, animals, the earth and all its many miracles. Goddess worship brings to light and celebrates all that mysterious, expansive, creative energy inside of you and lets the radiance of this become the measure of the quality of your life. A life that says "yes!" to life in all its cycles and states of becoming.

For a very long time, women were beguiled into thinking that once they got married they would live happily ever after. Now, more and more women know that this is not so and certainly that you can't trade off your own life for the married life and still feel alive. Marriages that start out as shelters eventually turn into sickbeds. Union with another is only exciting and meaningful when it is sacred and creative. When it is characterized by clinginess and unconscious routines, it is dead. Furthermore, because the intuitive, creative, feminine part of men's consciousness tends to be so understated, women who want to grow and live in a state of beauty, joy, wonder and possibility can only be frustrated, thwarted and denied if they are expecting marriage to bring all of this to them. This does not mean that they have to get divorced. It does mean that they have to find the Goddess power within themselves and in all kinds of relationships, experiences and involvements that have a soulful quality.

In ancient Greek temples, women initiated other women into the mysteries of womanhood. Through these rituals and practices they were made to feel the sacredness of their own bodies. Today, most women are ashamed of some part of their physique. The fitness craze is partially motivated by a sense of shame: If you don't work out and diet yourself into a socially approved shape, you're disgusting.

Goddess power is the opposite of shame. It involves an expansion of your unique emotional, spiritual, creative potential. The priceless by-product of that process is wisdom. The only protection we have against the painful surprises of life is wisdom: the higher, meaningful, intuitive understanding of truth. Not every woman can be the most cosmetically beautiful. But *every* woman can be wise. The wise Goddess within has all the answers. She is serene in the midst of chaos because she *understands*.

Goddess power comes from gaining this kind of consciousness that is light in the midst of darkness. It is also about healing, nurturing, replenishing and inspiring. I hope this book inspires you to be more alive, to understand more and to grow closer and closer to the beautiful, wise, mysterious and totally creative Goddess within you.

... if you travel far enough, one day you will recognize yourself coming down the road to meet yourself. And you will say—YES.

—Marion Woodman

FOR ALL SIGNS

The Goddess Gift:
The Sacred in the Everyday

LIFE IS SACRED. GODDESS POWER COMES TO THOSE WHO are conscious of that sacredness. It grows when you bring a sense of the sacred to the experience of the everyday so that living becomes a spiritual and creative act. Women who have a great deal of Goddess power know how to transform the mundane into the magical. There are a lot of ways to do this which I will discuss in this chapter. However, cultivating this spirituality is part of a process, a journey toward greater consciousness. This consciousness develops when you are able to see life in everything around you, to be receptive to it, taking it in through your heart and letting it move you, perhaps transform you. Along the path your eyes widen. One day they become new eyes that see more light, color and beauty than ever imagined. You are awake.

This reminds me of a friend who was in one of those bad places where it seems like life is a ten-foot-tall trench. Although she did have beauty in her life, her mind's dwelling place was on everything that on a daily basis she hated. One night she came for dinner and I was running late with the preparations. She asked if she could help and I told her that she could clip the stems of the roses and arrange them in their bowl. I paid no attention as she went about her task. However, later I was startled to see that she had stuffed them so unthinkingly into the bowl that they looked drunk. These roses were breathtaking in color, shape and smell but she didn't really see them. She didn't pay homage to their uniqueness. She didn't allow them to make a beautiful moment for her. Likewise, in her own life, she ran past so many potentially magical moments, letting the obsessions of her mind cloud and contract the life that was all around her.

We all have demons and problems and fears that diminish our joy in life, making it sometimes difficult to see the beauty of what is in front of us. However, when you are wise you know that these dark places are merely a part of the journey, not a stopping point. With this attitude, you look for the meaning of situations in your life and you have the full expectation that you will find it and it will be illuminating. The purpose of this book is to present this awareness and help you achieve this attitude which will be a light on the path of your life. Our demons and disappointments can lead us to more light if we know how to go deep within ourselves—our authentic, unique selves to find it. We all have this inner light and by coming together and sharing stories about its transformational power we increase its strength.

This book hopefully serves the function of a sharing experience. When you read along, pretend you are listening to a friend who sees what you can't see and knows what you have yet to know. It is critically important to see—to see all the wonderful things that you are and that you can be and also to look for the incredible potential in others. The key to spiritual transformation is developing a relationship with your inner world that becomes increasingly rich and meaningful with time so that its wisdom sustains and uplifts you.

We need to nourish our lives and our inner lives to enable them to flower. Here are some suggestions that will help you open your eyes and see the beauty that surrounds you. Some of these ways are simple, others are more involved. Do as many as you can, all the while keeping in mind that you're using these exercises with the goal of increasing your Goddess power.

1. Create Beauty

• Buy fresh flowers for yourself. If they are fragrant, smell them several times a day.

• Eat your meals by candlelight—even if you are eating alone. Put flowers on the table. Create a setting that's worthy of a goddess.

• Wear your clothes and makeup to show off what you find beautiful about yourself. Especially if it's raining or dark and miserable, wear something bright, colorful, and if you have the courage, startling!

• If you are in a bad mood that you can't shake, buy one beautiful thing for your living space that you *love* to look at.

• Buy a wonderful fish, bird, cat or dog. A wonderful pet can brighten your life with its personality and love.

2. Create a Sacred Living Space

If you live alone, decorate your space in a way that nourishes your soul. Enhance color and your favorite possessions. Make it a place that you love to come home to. This does not require a lot of money. It does, however, require imagination. If you feel you don't have that much imagination, be patient, experiment and give yourself some time. You'll be surprised what you come up with if you really let yourself go. If you live with someone, create a space for yourself that uplifts you. Use flowers (fresh or dried), inspirational books, poetry, candles, your own handmade artifacts or your favorite mementos.

3. Be Creative

• Write poetry or short stories or keep a journal

• Paint

• Color

• Do collages

• Sculpt

• Write music or songs

• Draw

• Make a wreath or special flower arrangements

• Do needlepoint

- Do woodwork or stenciling
- Create a garden
- Cook a beautiful dinner just for yourself!

Extend yourself by expressing yourself. It doesn't matter how you do that or how good you are. What matters is how it makes you feel, how the act itself frees you from the immediacy of the mundane and puts you in an emotional space that is sacred and uniquely you. If you make a habit of these self-enhancing activities, you will begin to trust what is inside you and you will become confident that it is *always* there for you to return to. Creativity is an important part of godliness. As such, it is a portal to your own hidden potential.

4. Create Sacred Moments

Your special time might be tea by the fire, a solitary walk in the woods, a bath by candlelight with strains of Mozart in the background. There are so many sacred moments you can create if you put your mind and heart to it. The more sacred moments that you create for yourself, the more sacred your life becomes. Since I've moved to Connecticut, one of my favorite sacred moments is listening to the rain quietly patter on the trees while surrounded by my silly Persian cats, stretched out and smiling in their sleep. When I lived in New York and I had a bad day, I would make a roaring fire in the fireplace, light candles on the mantel and all over the living room and blare my favorite Bach violin concerto. This helped me transcend the day's negativities. It also gave me a feeling that I was in my own self-created church. Whatever your specific sacred moments are, they should kindle your spirit and cause you to say "yes!" to life.

5. Get Close to Nature

Nature contains the magic of the Goddess. The life in grass, trees and gardens is sacred. The sounds of wind, water and trees rustling are an open meditation. Those sounds can quiet the jangle of your mind so that your deep inner intuitive voice will flow through. It is interesting how so many pressing problems and persistent annoyances seem so petty or simply disappear when you are staring at the mysterious, crashing surf or sitting on the forest floor in stillness, looking up at the sun filtering through the treetops. During such quiet, reflective moments you experience your higher self. Your higher self is that part of you that is connected to nature and all living things. The sounds of the forest and the sea are alive and will speak to that spiritual side of you if you relax for a moment.

6. Read Spiritual Books and Reflect on Them

Reading spiritual books can help you open doors of awareness and perception. Not only do we need new insights, we also have to be reminded of wise and important things we already know. I am both amused and disconcerted when I read something insightful I wrote in an earlier book and say to myself, "I wrote that?!" wondering how I could have forgotten it. We all forget and need to be reminded of the sacred within us and around us. Reading a book like *Living With Joy*, channeled by Sanaya Roman, immediately puts me in touch with the brightest part of myself and shows me I can dwell there. I carry around important quotations in my bag and refer to them throughout the day. Do this with any spiritual book that seems to speak to you and the issues in your life.

7. *Process Happenings/Incorporate Insights*

When you come upon your meaningful spiritual insights, you have to live them. That's the hardest part. This is particularly difficult for air signs (Gemini, Libra, Aquarius), who are quick to grasp a point but often keep it trapped in their heads. The prime way of incorporating insights in order to bring about emotional change is to live consciously and think on the meaning of things. Everything that affects you has a message, and the painful experiences often have the richest messages of all. Once you harvest this message and act on it, your life changes for the better, even if that change begins as just a little shift at first. All you need is one little positive change to start the process. However, keep in mind that understanding the message can often be difficult. There are some messages that come to you in a few hours or days of reflection. There are others that take years. Sometimes you cannot achieve the understanding of a painful experience until you have transformed as a person. Nevertheless, if you focus on finding the meanings in life experiences, you *will* grow and you will be able to gain from circumstances which would otherwise be considered merely miserable. Everything is a garden door to be opened when you find the right key. Some keys take a long time to be found. Others are right there before you. Regardless of what you might think, your circumstance, however painful or mundane it might seem, is magical. It is speaking to you. You just have to develop an ability to reflect upon daily occurrences and grasp the meaning for you in each one of them.

8. Keep a Journal

Journals are wonderful for two reasons. First, they make you see, reflect and become more aware of everything around you and how it affects you. Second, journals are extremely illuminating when you read back over them and see how you've grown spiritually compared to an earlier time in your life. Journals record our inner world. They speak a lot of inner truths that the conscious mind hasn't yet awakened to. One woman I knew kept going back and forth over her troubled feelings regarding her relationship right before her wedding but decided to get married anyway. Denying her negative feelings, she entered into a marriage that was disastrous and emotionally and financially costly. One day, reading an old journal, she was shocked to see the rage, misery and distrust she felt for this man. Had she faced these truths, she would not have had to experience the very painful lesson of her failed marriage. Some miserable lessons are not necessary. They happen because we're not consciously facing and understanding the message life is offering us.

9. Trust Your Feelings/Affirm Yourself

You were born with one big advantage in the game of life: woman's intuition. Use it. Don't block your feelings and throw yourself headlong into the fire. It hurts. Trust your gut feelings, instincts and intuitions in all relationships. Scene: You're in a situation with a man. He says something that hurts or embarrasses you. Address it. Don't pretend you didn't hear it. By acting on that feeling, your Goddess intelligence is affirming yourself. If you are strongly attracted to a man but your little voice is whispering "don't trust," *trust* your instinct! Denying it can get you into deep trouble. On the other hand, going with your gut instinct helps you affirm who you are. Every time you act from self-affirmation, you act from power. It's this kind of power that's going to determine the quality of your life. Therefore, own your own power and act from your instinctual intelligence, not ignorance or denial.

10. Chart Your Cycles

Women are mysterious lunar creatures. Their consciousness, like the cycles of the moon, is in constant flux. The bodies of women go by monthly cycles that also have emotional overtones. Furthermore, women's bodies follow a life cycle defined by the years of menstruation and the ones defined by menopause. On a daily basis, there are moods and/or feeling fluctuations. Notice if there is a time of the month, not necessarily your period, when you are emotionally dark or need to withdraw. Are these periods all alike, or if they differ, how do they differ? Delve into them. What illuminations come to the surface? Paint your mood. What do you see? What is its message? Write a poem inspired by your visual reaction to your painting.

Some women live on a purely external level, much the same as men. They go to the office and the gym, discuss clothes, men and work with their friends and that's it. The Goddess points to the richness—the brilliance, God-given creativity and wisdom that are on the inside needing to come out. This exercise is one way to make contact with your own magical inner kingdom that can so easily be strangulated by the deadness of a purely outwardly focused daily routine.

11. Self Talk

As women we all have that voice inside our heads that shrieks disgust at body parts or performance that is less than perfect. Usually that voice becomes so familiar it is like an alter ego. The danger is that the discomfort these negative thoughts create becomes too comfortable. We are mortified by an extra five pounds. We make jokes about physical attributes that we feel have failed us. And then there is the business of fear. That fearful voice in our heads has an extensive vocabulary. Language is very powerful—whether it is spoken or unspoken. We become what we tell ourselves we are. Therefore, it is very important to tell ourselves positive things. Remember that Goddess power grows out of an expansion of our spirit and being, not diminishment. And you can begin to create this expansion through how you emotionally feed yourself. Feed yourself compliments for all of your positive qualities. Spend some time thinking about your worthy acts. Take joy in them. Cultivating the Goddess within you is about appreciating your life and knowing that your life is sacred.

12. Sharing

Connection with quality people is what gives life its vitality, and sharing our feelings, fears, joys and insights with other women is a spiritual act. There is the joy-filled sharing of close friends. There is also the affirmative sharing within groups that serves to verify our personal experiences. The sense of going somewhere exciting inside yourself, becoming that creative, independent, free person you always wanted to be and sharing that expectation on a regular basis with others can be an extremely enlivening addition to your daily life.

Create a Goddess group (which can be as small as just you and one friend) that meets every week over wine and cheese or a candlelit meal that you all prepare together. Use this Goddess group for support, sharing, mutual inspiration, meditation, and spirituality. Through it, help each other see and live through the sacred in the everyday. Have everyone come with a quotation, paragraph or book that has inspired them that week. Be ready to share with the group one wonderful, meaningful growth experience that happened to you during that week. This kind of practice is an eye-opener. It makes you alert to the magic of your own life. And the more we start to see and expect, the more wonderful things we will receive on a daily basis.

13. Take Time to Withdraw

Periodic withdrawal can be both nurturing and healing. The late psychiatrist Esther Harding compared women's monthly cycle to the moon's cycle. Every woman has a new moon phase, a full moon phase and a dark of the moon phase. She said that the time of a woman's period is analogous to the dark of the moon phase and that a woman "has an opportunity at the dark of the moon to get in touch with a deeper and more fundamental layer of her own psychic life. Symptoms of physical or emotional disturbance at that time indicate that there is a conflict between her conscious attitude and the demands of her own nature, and if she recognizes them as an indication of her need to be by herself, because an inner necessity is calling to her to withdraw psychologically from the demands of her external life and live for a little while in the secret places of her own heart, she may be able to reestablish her contact with the deeper part of her own nature."

To turn within—aided perhaps by beautiful music or total silence, to read poetry or a spiritually uplifting book, reflect, make connections, dwell on meanings, write—can be emotionally and spiritually rejuvenating. When you are able to create quiet, meditative places for yourself, at any time of the month, you are able to access the domain of the Goddess. It is a mysterious, creative space of emotional/psychic possibility. And as Harding said, "The important thing is . . . that we should each create something which did not exist before, (to) unfold the latent power of creator which slumbers within us, for this is our most godlike faculty."

This is the power of the Goddess. Every woman has this tremendous gift at her disposal. Discover it. Make an adventure of this discovery in your own life and in the process make every day sacred.

ARIES
(March 21–April 20)

Your Essential Self

VIBRANT, ENERGETIC AND INTENSELY ALIVE, THE ARIES woman exudes a spirit that can be contagious. She is the first of the three fire signs and so there is a sort of childlike sense of immediacy which bursts forth from her. At times, her exuberance can take the form of a full-blown emotional naivete that can trip her up. At other times it is embodied in a supercharged enthusiasm and zest for whatever she is involved in. More than anything else, the Aries woman wants to feel hot with life. She wants to have intensity and interesting things to look forward to. Boredom is something she can't tolerate. She also can't tolerate anything that restricts her sense of spontaneity. She wants to feel wild and free, looking forward to a future that holds exciting surprises.

Ambitious, impatient and quick to rise to a challenge, she encounters life head-on. Smart and self-confident about her place in the scheme of things, the

Aries woman is a take-charge person who thrives in the role of leader. She loves the attention that goes with the spotlight and relishes the prospect of fame or being first in her chosen field. A superachiever who usually accomplishes a lot in life, she'll take on challenging projects that others would be quick to shy away from. At her best she can win battles with sharks and on a slow day is merely superproductive. Not at all shy about accepting praise, she will go out of her way to seek it. An initiator who never knows when to stop, her aim is always first place. Positive, assertive and always thinking in superlatives, she also has a great sense of timing and can get things done before others even realize there is anything to do. Then, with renewed vigor, she is off pursuing her next challenge.

Aries women have an instinctive sense of hierarchy and status. Easily impressed by wealth, success and social standing, they strive to create their own realm at the top and often cultivate relationships with people who are power connections. Aries is a restless, impatient sign that needs to keep moving. Physical activity is a must and a much needed outlet for megawatt energies. Athletic by nature and having a strong body consciousness, Aries women are often fitness fanatics who take great pride in their physical prowess.

Classic extroverts, Aries females like to conquer the world in a lot of ways and also to claim a big piece of it. Generous, often to a fault, they are quick to share their bounty. The Aries spirit gets even brighter through their ability to befriend and inspire those with less light, fewer gifts and less natural advantages. Their "can-do" approach can turn meager cabins into castles and transform potential pitfalls into award-winning performances. Aries represents perhaps the purest power of creation—the ability to have a vision, the initiative to act on it and the ability to make something wonderful from it. Whether they are creating a picture on a blank canvas or a business that grows into a corporation, the Aries spirit burns with fire from the Source. Wisely directed, this energy can be heroic, brimming with possibility and infused with the sort of inspiration that says "yes!" to life.

Your Dark Side

WHEN THE POWERFUL MARTIAN ENERGY IS TURNED INward and not focused in positive action, it can be a very destructive and unruly force. Depression, obsession, emotional instability and problems with alcohol or drugs are dangers that can face an Aries. The restless need for excitement can also lead to adolescent, addictive love relationships. Aries women need a lot of outlets for their energies. Exercise is always one of them. Sex is another. However, when the energies propel her in the direction of escapism, problems begin that can darken or destroy her.

Impulsive, impatient and demanding instant gratification, the Aries woman can act out both a selfishness and an emotional immaturity that makes her difficult to be around. There can be a "me first" or a "me, me, me" attitude to this sign that can dominate and alienate others. The difficult part of this is that this behavior is so unconscious that the perpetrator is never aware of how she affects others. And if her behavior is brought to her attention, it is likely that she would be both shocked and offended. For this reason it is important for the Aries woman to work on watching herself, hearing herself and being more conscious of the total effect of her behavior on others. Although she is very self-conscious, she is not always self-aware. And there is a big difference between these two states of mind. The Aries woman can easily project her own behavior onto the people close to her—when she doesn't see herself clearly. This emotional bind can be enhanced by her own tendency to act before she thinks. Being such an impulsive and impatient sign, it is not an Aries woman's nature to stop and analyze. However, it is something she can learn and master. And if she does, these efforts will make her a more powerful person.

Being such a dynamic sign is not always easy. Aries instincts have to be harnessed or else they can run roughshod over her whole personality and be damaging. This can be seen in thoughtless, insensitive and sometimes cruel behavior that is subjective and often self-serving. In its extreme, this negative behavior separates a woman from her own precious feminine source. She behaves like a power-oriented man who is prepared to ruthlessly push others too far to attain self-serving ends.

The Aries woman has to watch how she uses power. If she is power tripping and thinks she has the upper hand, it will eventually undermine her. And the chances are strong that when it does, she won't really understand what is happening or how she got there. Whether it is a mysterious depression, substance abuse or relationship problems, it will seem to her as if it just crept up and took over. The Aries woman owes it to herself to see that this doesn't happen. She owes it to herself to see that she lives a full life to the best of her potential and within that life, she is able to generate love, not diminish it. The woman born under this expansive sign must work at being aware and expand in the right direction. She can do this by focusing on raising her consciousness. This means taking time to analyze situations and slowing down just a bit to consider the meaning of them and her part in them.

Aries has a lot of needs—needs for love, attention, flattery, power and success. Gradually, these needs should be replaced by a self-esteem that is not dependent on adulation from the outside. An Aries driving herself for material power rather than personal meaning, will be doing everything for the wrong reason and will eventually trip herself up. There are women who grow old getting in their own way. An Aries woman doesn't want to be one of them. She should be conscious of who she uniquely is. If she asks herself the right questions, she will get the important answers and her life will be a rich unfolding that can become an interesting and meaningful adventure. It can also become authentic and creative and provide a power that is hers alone to claim.

Your Approach to Love

HIGHLY ROMANTIC AND SEXUAL, LOVE BEARS A GREAT deal of importance in the life of the Aries woman. Prone to impulsive, passionate encounters and amorous adventures, the Aries woman usually has more than her share of love affairs. The Aries Gloria Steinem is noted for her clever comment, "A woman without a man is a fish without a bicycle." The great irony, of course, is that in her life she is never without a man. Aries women never are. There may or may not be one steady, committed relationship but there is never a complete absence of men. Although Aries are independent in a lot of ways, emotionally they have an overwhelming need for a passionate connection. Highly flirtatious and very spontaneous, the Aries woman revels in the game of seduction and of course, the splendor of the courtship—which ideally has to be larger than life in some way to keep her interest. Usually, her greatest interest is that her lover's attention be focused fully on her. Aries women love being loved—perhaps even more than they love loving. However, it is also not uncommon to see this woman get completely hung up on some guy who is not really deserving and perhaps not completely attainable. A challenging man enhances the sense of romance in her eyes. Mars, her ruler, comes alive with conquest and sometimes this exacts a high price. And so, there can be a bit of that at work in the love life of this sign. There is also a desire for flash, glamour and power. Like her Leo sister, the Aries woman loves to mythologize her romance, making it a spectacle of the gods—the gods, of course, being herself and her lover.

Aries women believe in magic. This can be very charming. However, it can also lead to delusion and disillusionment when the prince starts croaking like the frog he always was. Aries and Leo women are often more in love with the drama of love than with any particular person—which they may not realize until they've been through quite a few love connections. At the same time, they are also able to generate a sense of excitement with the right person. However, the quiet, low-key, stay-at-home types need not get their hopes up. Aries women cannot tolerate anything low-key for long and when they really get restless, they can get really difficult. Being a fire sign, ruled by Mars, Aries emotions can burst into flame. Arien anger usually doesn't last long but can be a blowtorch at the time. Also, too much boredom with a lover can cause an Aries mind and body to drift in a new romantic direction. Once she is really bored, the fire goes out and the passion will never be quite the same. There has to be a certain amount of action and intensity to keep her fires flickering. This is not a sign that can stand too much banal routine or deadly quiet. A little immature? At times, perhaps. This is, after all, the very first of the twelve signs and one that takes some time growing up. When she does grow up, though, she is generous, expansive, loyal and loving, with an almost childlike innocence. The Aries woman is fully present in the moment, giving of herself with a pure, overflowing heart that is a power in and of itself, and a marvelous verification of what the human spirit can be.

Your Power Source

AT HER MOST POWERFUL, AN ARIES WOMAN IS WHAT I call "spacious." She is generous, expansive and inspiring. She is an enemy of the small-minded and the petty. But, even more important, she is able to act on her inner visions and dreams to bring about positive change.

The Aries female can be a crusader and champion of the underdog. And she can create great things out of nothing. When I say great things I mean everything from small, spontaneous acts of kindness to huge organizations and powerful reforms that change the quality of many people's lives.

The Aries woman can make what is dark and small, large, bright and shining. The key to all of this is not merely her energy. It is her attitude that says "yes, I will!" or "yes, I can!" The ability to say "yes!" to life despite odds, frustrations and setbacks is a gift that makes this sign shine. In the process of achieving huge things herself, she can be a great inspiration to others. She can help people believe in themselves and she can share some of her light in a way that enables others to change their life.

Because she sees the big picture and has no patience for petty obstacles that easily trip others up, she can be a highly magnanimous spirit who sails through the darkest of seas, ushering in the sun. The Aries woman must put her ideas and ideals into action so that her vision manifests itself outwardly. She has to reach beyond purely personal involvements to a wider concern for all life. She has so much to contribute in this rapidly changing world that is blighted with so much darkness. She can be such a bright light that she is capable of creating a global community or a major organization that revolutionizes how people think and behave. When she is able to get beyond her personal ego needs and acts from the power of her spirit, there is no stopping her and there is no end to her motivation or the vast outpouring of her energy.

Therefore, the woman born under this sign must always hold close to her heart the importance of her own growth and expansion. She must always challenge herself to see things in new ways that promote the highest values in herself and others. In order to experience her power fully, she must channel her passionate nature into powerful acts of spirit and kindness. At her best, the Aries woman is a brilliant light unto herself and as she radiates outward, she has the potential of positively motivating many people and making a big difference in their lives.

The Aries woman is capable of focusing on a piece of the world and making it so much better. The most wonderful thing is that in the process of contributing to the world in this dynamic way, she expands herself. Through the act of giving, she becomes greater and larger. This greatness is a powerful, mysterious force that will carry her through even in those darker times when she might feel merely mortal.

TAURUS
(April 21–May 21)

Your Essential Self

THERE IS SOMETHING PURE AND BASIC ABOUT TAURUS. Taurus is the first of the three earth signs and the one closely connected with the fertile aspect of spring. At this time of the year there are flowers that have forced their way through the earth to show their face to the sun. They feel the first essential warmth gracing the earth. The sun's rays, which nurture growth, become an intrinsic part of the life force of new living things.

Taurean women have a similar essential warmth. It is a guileless warmth, not effusive or showy, but gentle, calm and fully present. It is also patient, sometimes too patient.

Ruled by Venus, the planet of love and beauty, Taurean women need both of these qualities in their lives. They are the queens of creature comforts. Comfort and security are extremely important to them. And because Venus also has her self-indulgent aspects, Taurean women love luxuries, especially luxuries that are sensuous or that boast solid, impressive materialistic names like Armani or Ferrari.

And then there is that subject of love. Taurean women need love or what appears to their senses as love, often to the exclusion of needing themselves as independent individuals. Romantic, sensual love, with all the best material trappings makes them starry-eyed. So does the language of love. Taurus women take romantic words for everlasting truth. They are old-fashioned romantics who would like to think that a hero is hanging around in the great unknown getting himself ready to appear and make her dreams come true.

Unfortunately, real life is not so cozy or rosy. We must take care of ourselves if we are to have any personal power. However, Taurus women do love the idea of a very rich man supporting them and many put their energies toward accomplishing this goal. In the natural horoscope, Taurus rules the second house of money, values and self-value. In this sign, all three are intrinsically tied together. Taurean women value money so much that it becomes a reflection of their own self-value. Taurean women tend to see their worth in two respects: through their material base and through their love connection. A Taurean woman who has neither does not feel secure and must compensate through nurturing herself in creative and spiritual ways.

The classic Taurean woman knows that nurturing is essential to life. Taurus is a feminine sign, which means it is slower in rhythm, receptive rather than generative and more involved with process than the sun signs that represent active masculine energy. A Taurus woman nurtures herself through food, fabrics, scents and a comfortable environment. However, she can also nurture herself through crafts, gardening, writing, woodworking and music. The Taurus woman has a sense of quality for quality's sake. Whether politically correct or not, she loves the feeling of being enclosed in fur on a bitter cold day. She loves top-grade leather, its look, smell and touch. She loves certain designers for the line of their clothes and quality of construction. Being a true sensualist, she understands the power of scent to transport the psyche to another place and time. The classic Taurus woman lives in her body. She loves baths and to be touched by the right person. She is also a purely sexual creature who thrives on lovemaking.

The problem comes when a Taurus allows herself to be enslaved by her senses. Taurean women have an obsessive quality. They can also behave very unconsciously in the throes of an intense love connection. When this happens, the Taurus woman becomes deaf to her own self-protective instincts as well as to intervening rational voices from the outside. The Taurus woman can be both stubborn and bullish about holding her ground, no matter what the cost. For this reason, at some time in her life, she is often shattered into consciousness through some devastating hurt. Unfortunately, however, being a sign of fixed earth, Taurus women often forget their life lessons and backslide into the same old undermining patterns. This is not only because of their rigidity but also because of their needs. The Taurean's need for love and sex can be so great that it dwarfs the person, replacing a healthy sense of self with a persistent hunger.

Taurean women are slow to learn emotionally and even slower to make changes. Being a fixed sign, they will do the same thing over and over again—go back to the same abusive person, hang on to the words of the slick, soulless man, and allow themselves to be hurt again through another round of cruel, disparaging behavior. Taurean women often mistake sex for connection. They can also confuse prosperity with quality and are particularly vulnerable to men in power.

Although there is a type of Taurean woman who is a basic earth mother, in tune with nature and her own nature, like the wonderful writer, May Sarton, many Taurus women are more caught up in the material sphere. Taurean women resonate to the culture's definition of power. Famous names, impressive labels, titles and status in any form makes many Taureans feel elevated and more worthwhile.

The problem with assigning such power to the outer world is that it denies the soul. And when the Taurus woman gets older and she judges her life and worth by standards that are not her own, standards that she has adopted from society, she will be living increasingly in a place that is not authentic. As teenagers, we are all influenced by those around us and many times conform to fashion. However, to have power as women we have to live to the best of our ability through our unique selves. We have to individualize. We have to make choices from the complex whole of ourselves, *not* from things or people outside of ourselves. Otherwise, our center becomes a void and the self, a self that has to be escaped from. The Taurean's desperate seeking of unconsciousness, whether it be through sex, love, food, TV, drugs, alcohol, computer screens or shopping, will have a diminishing effect on her life.

Unconsciously, our psyches seek wholeness, even if our search for it initiates crisis. The soul craves aliveness, not things. It yearns to be touched by the miracle of life. It doesn't care about the power of Wall Street or Hollywood, although the ego may care excessively. However, the soul is nourished by what is alive, be it a flower, the ocean, or a human heart that is unbearably beautiful.

If they choose to feel fully alive, Taurean women have to become acquainted with and start to live through their unique spirit. They have to want to see more, hear more and feel more within themselves instead of losing themselves in someone or something outside of themselves. This process, this growth, is the attainment of Goddess power. The other is a mechanical mind that is fueled by inertia. Nonthinking, repetitive patterns reduce life. Life should be dynamic and free-flowing. It should have an aim of being vital instead of being fixed and moving through this world's experiences unconsciously. This is what those women born under the sign of Taurus should remember and act from.

I think of one Taurus woman I knew who was in her forties and very depressed. Her world was flat, colorless and repetitive and she was certain that this was due to some cruel act of God. She had her own highly successful business but it didn't give her the sort of status that she craved. What she wanted was to be a famous Hollywood person like many of those she had known. She had grown up in Beverly Hills and her values remained power-oriented, movie star values. Along the way, she added materialistic Wall Street values to the list of things that influenced her behavior. Unfortunately, she never developed her own spiritual values and subsequently her life was completely meaningless, sparked only by the changes in the stock market and her next clothes purchase. Every Saturday, she dressed up in her perfect clothes and went shopping in the Madison Avenue designer boutiques. This was the high point of her week. The aura of chronic depression and spiritual deadness that surrounded this woman was so powerful that it was almost visible. This is what becomes of us when we ignore our soul. Life is dead and that deadness is spiritual pollution.

Taurus is a very creative sign and the creativity can have an outlet in writing, painting, crafts or carpentry. The ruler of this sign, Venus, is the ruler of all art forms. Venus is also the planet of love. Taurean women can be warm, loving people and wonderful mothers. However, they have to be careful to love from a place of strength, not neediness. The Taurean strength and patience can be healing and generative of powerful human connections. Likewise, the creativity could be an endless source of wonder and magic that continually expands her life. When the Taurus woman starts to explore who she is as well as who she might be, when she sees herself as a Source of unfolding potential, she is beginning to live from her own Goddess power. When heavy-duty ego considerations are replaced by the spontaneity of her own heart and humble respect for life, she is on her own path, a path that is unique to her. The desire to control or manipulate for personal gain is replaced by the ability to live simply from the heart. Now there is a deep reverence for life rather than a grasping need for ego affirmation. Instead of deadness that has to be escaped from, there is a vitality, a sense of connectedness to others and one's own spirit which makes a Taurean feel young, regardless of physical age. The Taurean woman who has tapped her spring of spiritual life is receptive to life and nature. She cares about the earth, not just her bank account. She wants to give something to society, rather than be in need of society's approval. She generates love from her expansive heart instead of feeling empty and lovelorn. Instead of emptiness, there is a consciousness, and it is quiveringly alive and ever changing. The Taurus woman who is in touch with her Goddess energy views her own life as a creation, a precious creation that is always teaching her something, ever leading her to greater meaning, depth and a wisdom that is divine.

Your Dark Side

THE HARDEST THING IN THE WORLD FOR A TAURUS woman to do is to let go. Slow to change her mind or her emotional fixation, she can be both stubborn and inflexible. This, needless to say, gets in the way of her being able to see the higher value of experience. It can also bind her to the wrong things, ideas or people that can take away her power.

To benefit most from her life, the Taurus woman should always try to challenge herself to see things in new ways, to see more, to go farther. The deadly pitfall of Taurus is the rut that only gets deeper with time. The life of the rut is a mechanical life, a life without consciousness or deep, changing, evolving meaning. This is a deadened life, a life with no possibility.

Taurus women are often too slow to grasp what they can do to extricate themselves from a bad situation. Often, it takes them a very long time to even admit there is a problem in their life. They tend to cling tighter and tighter to the problem that is strangling them, often until something inside of them or outside of them finally breaks. On this issue, there is a favorite story of mine that I always refer to as the Shelf story.

Sally was a strikingly beautiful woman. She was also an impeccable housekeeper who put perhaps too much attention on perfecting all the little mundane details of her life. Her focus was always on the small matters. She never looked at the big picture or the deeper picture. One day her neighbor came in and saw Sally perched on a stepladder straining to dust a high shelf that was already gleamingly free of dust. Curious, she asked her what she was doing. Sally replied that her husband told her that if she were a better housekeeper he would make love to her. What she did not get was that he was impotent and could not make love to her. However, he was also smart and saw how he could easily manipulate that situation so that she would think it was her problem—which she most definitely did.

Another dark area in the life of a Taurus woman is anger, an anger based on their subjective sense of like and dislike, an anger that denies mature communication. Here, the Taurus woman is quick to act out in primitive, punishing ways, rather than see the picture as a complex whole and her part in it. There is a very destructive sense of self-righteousness in this sign that denies truth and can be highly tyrannical. This is also a sign that tends to have emotional hearing problems. The Taurus woman needs to develop her ability to listen and really hear, to hear beyond her own subjective superficial take. One way of doing this is to care enough to ask questions and take the conversation further. However, as is often the case, her focus is on what she is saying and wants to say. If the Taurus woman did develop the ability to hear what was being said between the lines (a true Goddess power), then she would have a much deeper understanding of others' complexities. This, in turn, could make her own life larger. This largesse would bring her to a level of human compassion that would encourage the potential in situations and people, regardless of what she might see through her mere subjectivity. It is here especially that the Taurus woman needs to get unstuck.

The Taurus woman has a tendency to hold on to grudges and negative emotional attitudes after life has changed all around her. People change, governments change, countries change and the Taurus woman is still holding on to her phantoms of thoughts and feelings. I think of this stubbornness as someone sitting for days in a car that has run out of gas. Because the car once had gas, the person just keeps sitting there relying on it to be a viable mode of transportation. Eventually the car rusts and the body disintegrates but the person just keeps sitting there in the driver's seat, going nowhere, not comprehending that there is nowhere to go in this particular vehicle.

Just as cars need fuel, people need to forgive, forget and forge ahead. Even on a molecular level, life is about movement and change. The Taurus woman needs to do emotional and spiritual overhauls on a regular basis. She needs to clean out her emotional closets and throw some things away, or else she will be throwing away potentially meaningful parts of her life. She needs to look at herself and others in a larger, more expansive way—a view that comes from the heart, not the ego. She needs to remain open—open to change, open to what she is not seeing or hearing—so that more will come in. If the Taurean woman does this, she won't become shut down or cut off from the good that could come in. Finally, the Taurus woman must value herself enough to be completely honest with herself—no matter how much that might hurt. The Taurean has to look at what she is really doing with her own life. Is she living it, is she denying it, is she cutting parts of it off that she doesn't want to face? Here, a wonderful line from the ancient Chinese sage Confucius comes to mind, "There is the closest connection between the skilled archer and the person of true nobility. When she misses the target, she looks for the cause in herself."

Your Approach to Love

LOVE, SEX AND ROMANCE ARE EXTREMELY IMPORTANT for the Taurus woman. The typical Taurus woman assigns a lot of power to the opposite sex, sometimes so much power that men can take on a larger-than-life significance. Taurus women often cast men into roles such as heroes or villains or keepers of the gate of an ideal way of life. The men who fall between the cracks are the ones who are less visible. The Taurus woman loves to think of her man in an archtypal way: strong, supersmart (smarter than she is), heroic and someone who looks good in the world at large and makes her look good by association. There is a great temptation to cast a man into a mold onto which she projects her own talents and fantasies. This can be very dangerous when it goes so far that the Taurean doesn't see her man for himself and reduces him to the part that she wants him to play in her life. In this sort of situation, years can pass and the man may have changed so much that he is no longer the same person. However, she will remain steadfast in trying to hold him to the role that he has long ago outlived, if he, in fact, ever really lived it at all.

Whether male or female, it takes Taurus a very long time to learn life's lessons, especially in love. In a relationship where she is being treated as less than a worthwhile human being, the Taurus woman will often remain loyal and endure further mistreatment. In a situation where it is clear that the man has become indifferent to her, her tendency will be to rationalize and wait for things to get better. Too much waiting and conditions start to get the better of her. Still, Taurus will wait years. The Taurus woman is an old-fashioned romantic who often values men more than women. The women who have grown and gotten beyond this kind of thinking are the ones who are really capable of loving because they have come to love and value themselves. This kind of Taurus woman—who thinks for herself—lives out the positive attributes of her ruler Venus. The love she is capable of is rich, nourishing and nurturing. However, she is also capable of nurturing herself and sees that as a value.

The Taurus woman needs a lot of emotional and sexual love and she delights in returning the gestures of affection. She can be very pure and genuine and offer overflowing love from her heart. However, there is also another kind of Taurus woman who is very manipulative and calculating. She can appear to be caring while working toward her own selfish ends. Taurus women want terribly to be liked and to look good in the eyes of the beholder. The manipulative Taurus woman always has her ego gratification in mind.

Despite the fact that security and stability are so important to her, especially in her early life, the Taurus woman is often attracted to men who are exciting and selfish rather than caring. Often they are freedom-loving fire signs (Aries, Leo, Sagittarius). However, the emotionally enigmatic water signs (Cancer, Scorpio, Pisces) also have their strong and sometimes dangerous allure for her.

The Taurus woman must endure a lot of lessons in love, most of which revolve around discrimination and misplaced trust. She tends to project onto men highly attractive qualities which she herself possesses, but that she is not owning and living out consciously. Therefore, often the power, fame, flair or accomplishments of the man become a substitute for her own meaningful self-determined action. She tends not to value her own talents and abilities as much as she values being someone's lover or wife. Self-discovery is not her strong suit. Therefore reflection, analysis and a lot of work on discovering the meaning of her life experiences—understanding what they are trying to tell her—are essential, if she is ever to consciously own the power of her own soul. She has to be aware that emotional and sexual neediness can cut her off from a spiritually authentic experience of her own life.

We all have needs. However, neediness is often the symptom of a deeper issue. It is often the indication of a void on the inside that insists on being filled up by someone or something on the outside. Goddess power involves filling that void in creative ways that are extensions of oneself rather than escapes from oneself. That does not mean taking up painting as a substitute for a love relationship. It does mean trying to become more whole in a lot of ways, discovering and expressing yourself so that love, when it comes, is about partnership, not a desperate solution to personal loneliness or emptiness. When a Taurus woman is conscious, she will attract a more conscious man and the relationship will reflect her positive self-value. She will be able to discriminate. She will be able to tell the good guys from the bad guys and won't be easily blown out of the water by a man's superficial qualities alone. She may say to herself—well he's very interesting and attractive but I also see problems here. She will know and expect real quality in a person and she will help encourage that through her own consciousness. Finally, she will be living a much more vital and meaningful existence defined by this positive self-value instead of slowly dying inside while holding on to some fantasy.

In the meantime, to throw oneself away to or squander one's energies on an inappropriate situation is an improper and tragic sacrifice of self. To have a romantic relationship, one should never sacrifice one's self or soul. This kind of behavior is appropriate for teenage love. However, to continue to do so as an adult woman is both neurotic and terribly immature.

Taurus is ruled by the planet Venus. Venus represents two levels of living. On the lower level, it represents self-indulgent pleasure and on the higher level, the powerful, transformative mystery of love. Taurus women need to be Goddesses unto themselves, for themselves. They need to be touched by the power of their own soul and to allow it to lead them to their own unfolding mystery as it lights the way to the wisdom and potential joy of their own hearts.

Your Power Source

THE GREAT POWER SOURCE OF THE TAURUS WOMAN IS her heart and her ability to love. At her best, she is guileless and sincere. It is the combination of this heartfelt response and her ability to show her feelings with such deep warmth that can make her a substantial human being in a very superficial world. Deep personal caring is her essence. Venus, her ruler, is the planet of love and when her focus is on giving out rather than grasping and pulling in, she can be a powerful embodiment of the heart chakra.

The Taurus woman is steadfast, loyal and patient, especially with those she loves. Her natural stability makes her someone who is there when needed, someone who can be counted on, regardless of her own priorities and problems. She is a constant in her loving response and can be a very calming influence in a crisis.

I remember a favorite aunt who was a Taurus. She was completely there for me through my teen and college years when my relationship with my own mother was rocky. She was probably the center of the family, the emotional ballast, who also had a positive effect on her self-involved sisters. Sunday dinner at her house was a source of nurturance that went straight to the soul. As a human being she was bountiful, yet she certainly had her own share of personal problems. These she faced one by one, always with a sense of humor and a philosophical bent that was truly inspiring. In the midst of a crisis she acted from practicality rather than emotion, although she was sensitive and felt everything very deeply. When I needed someone to talk to, she was the one. Even in the middle of the night, she was always there for me. Everyone loved to be around her because of the quiet, comfortable atmosphere of love she exuded.

My aunt could transform darkness into light and she did it in all different kinds of ways. A most magical memory of her was on a hot summer night when she came up with a wonderful thing to do. She, my cousin and myself went to the back lawn, near the woods, took our shoes off and danced in the dewy grass. She brought us Goddess magic. Although I was only nine or ten years old at the time, I will never forget the surge of life that coursed through me that night that said something loudly: "You are alive!" That night I deeply felt the wonder of my own life and a great appreciation for it. The earth, of course, is the domain of Taurus. I see Taurus women who are deadened and a little depressed because they have gotten so caught up in material power values that they manipulate rather than act from the heart. When I pass these women I think to myself how much they need to return to Mother earth and surrender to her power in order to get back in touch with the wonder of themselves. Whether they take strength from the ocean, the dewy grasses of a summer night, the stillness of the woods, or the peace that comes from sitting by a rushing stream—it is all the Goddess earth, the ancient archetypal domain of Taurus. The natural world has messages to give the Taurus woman through its effect on her unconscious.

Just as a return to nature simplifies the complications we create with our minds, Taurus women have a wonderful way of simplifying things, breaking them down into little pieces that are more easily dealt and dispensed with. Part of this ability comes from being practical and quickly seeing the bottom line. When this ability is used constructively and conscientiously, it can be a marvelous tool for eliminating a lot of negative emotional stuff that can weigh one down and hold one back. For instance, I have a Taurus friend who uses this ability to work on her own tendency to hold on to garbage from the past and be grudge-bearing. Recently she applied this to a very challenging situation in her life which involved her ex-husband and a woman, who was supposedly a friend, who seduced him. In an open, honest talk with this woman, a talk from her heart, this Taurus dispensed with all the old baggage, putting it where it belonged—out of a space in her mind. She realized that to continue to live with something that happened in the past as if it still had value in the present was a tremendous negative concentration of her own precious energy, when she wanted only to experience her own positive energy. When she related this experience to me, I became very still, as if I had suddenly stumbled upon something very sacred—and I had. It was the power of what a Taurus heart can be. I could clearly see that she was empowered by her realization and ability to act on it successfully. Consequently I felt a surge of enormous respect for her.

Taurus is the sign of spring—the new flowering of life. The Taurus women who live in this chosen place of renewal don't hold on to things that no longer exist.

Life changes. People change just as the seasons change. The powerful Taurus woman knows that and respects it. It is part of her wisdom. Living through her heart, she will always be able to flower with new feelings, attitudes and a life force that affirms herself and those around her. Her heart is a persuasive power, and how she shares it with the world will become its own reward.

GEMINI

(May 22–June 21)

Your Essential Self

GEMINI WOMEN HAVE A SCINTILLATING MENTAL EN-
ERGY. Most of them know it and use it to their advantage. Smart, cerebral, clever, witty and imaginative,
they make immediate connections—with people,
ideas, subjects, concepts and trends. It is this quality of
immediacy that gives Geminis their sparkle and makes
them such interesting companions. They are interested
people. They see a lot and they want to see more, and
that inspires them to look, learn, be open and inquire.

Gemini women are quick studies with fast, glib answers. Like everything, this is both good and bad. The
good side of this is that they initially make a favorable
impression on the world. The negative part is that
they tend to stick with first impressions that are often
superficial. Here, they cheat themselves—and others,
by not delving deep enough to grasp a more complex
picture of a person or situation. Having a quickly fad-
ing attention span, they quickly move on to the next

image on their mental screen, trusting what they see is the complete truth.

We all have to live through our essential nature, but we can also hone that down and improve it so that it works as a source of power rather than limitation. Being the best quality of ourselves *for ourselves* is the challenge of our life and the door to its unique meaning. The degree to which a Gemini woman allows herself to be cut off and stay cut off is the degree to which she is blocking her own possibility and emotional, intellectual and physical vitality. When her thinking process stays on a shallow level and starts to replace feeling, a slow, insidious emotional trap starts to close in. Life becomes routine, repetitious, mechanical, empty, constricted and draining. The mind needs to slow down. The superficial business needs to be put in its place so that its place does not become the entire scope of the mind. Therefore, a Gemini woman must stay intellectually open and reflective and not be so quick to trust that things are as obvious as they may seem. Our minds play tricks on us. A powerful, wise woman knows that and learns to hear with her heart and sense with her body. Our minds can make fools out of us when we are so willing to assign them total power. Therefore, the person, who at first glance, looks so weak or unappealing, may simply be a poor communicator with an intensely demanding inner world. So, judging others according to strictures of the outer world and sticking to those first impressions can be both dangerous and unfortunate for all concerned. It does make for a tidy picture but there are no tidy pictures in the world of people. Furthermore, everything is always changing, as the Gemini woman herself should know.

When the Gemini woman is able to slow herself down, to try to feel things with her heart and deeper sensibilities, then she is on the way to living in her higher power, her Goddess wisdom power. Gemini is the sign of personality and communication. That power is already there at birth but how it is used can keep expanding so that life expands and becomes a continual adventure. Because Gemini is the sign associated with the logical mind, what comes most naturally is to live through that. Knowledge and learning are so important that new knowledge that is accrued starts to feel personal, like it is a part of the self, an extension of the identity and ego. That is why extensive degrees and accomplishments take on such value. I think, therefore I am, becomes the source of power. However, as women, we are more than mental accomplishments. We are complex, mysterious, ever unfolding beings who need to breathe through the creative parts of ourselves. The more creative we are, the more centered the focus and the less prone to nervous maladies and insomnia (a chronic Geminian problem.) Insomnia takes over when the mind is scattered, obsessive and out of control. We are never fully present when the mind is in this state, however, when we are being creative we are fully present. The annoying jangle in the head is gone and there is a flow of energy that is intuitive, not purely mental. That intuitive voice is the source of brilliance and wisdom. It is the voice of the most important answers that are within as well as of the questions that really need to be answered.

There is nothing a Gemini loves more than having all the answers. The problem is that when the mind is operating on a superficial level, often she doesn't even know the right questions—the questions that have to be answered before moving forward in herself and her relationships. The Gemini woman must always be willing to go deeper if she is to grow as a feminine source of power. She must also be able to get beyond her restless mind to a source of Truth deep within herself that sustains her instead of looking to what's outside of herself for a confirmation of herself. Mercury, the ruling planet of Gemini, was known to be the great messenger of the gods. Its most profound lesson is about how we can communicate with ourselves in a manner that will enable us to connect with our own divinity. Gemini women have to be aware of how they communicate. When cut off from their deeper feelings, their brains take over like annoying, buzzing bees. The thoughts are like static electricity. The result is restless, fragmented mind that skirts the surface of experience.

This type of Gemini talks *at* others, not *to* them. There is a compulsive need to talk without an awareness of how it is being received. True communication is sharing, not constant chatter. There is a pacing. There are pauses that allow the other person to unfold. The wise Gemini woman is in the habit of listening to herself, hearing her words as they come out and taking responsibility for the power of her delivery. She is able to help the other person connect instead of merely releasing her own nervous energy.

Gemini women need to experience wonder. Their great lesson is their own power to create it. It all lies in their marvelous, God-given ability to communicate, a gift that can make others feel as if they've suddenly sprouted wings.

For the fullest range of communication, the Gemini

woman needs to hear her nonrational, intuitive voice. Furthermore, she has to come to trust it. However, logical Mercury, her ruling planet, tends to take over and get completely in the way of that. Mercury brings in so many rapid thoughts that the intuitive powers which require centeredness and a certain degree of mental quiet don't have much opportunity to make themselves noticed. It's very much like being lost on a road that is vaguely familiar and trying to decide at some point whether you should take a right or a left. The intuitive mind won't think about it. It will feel the left. But the logical mind will say, "I think I should take a left, but, no, it has to be a right because that road should connect me with the road I want."

When we follow Mercury's voice in intuitive situations we get lost. This lost dilemma can lead to further confusion if we rely on Mercury to sort it all out and set us straight. Mercury reigns over the mundane details and pragmatic facts of life. Being a smart Mercurial sort will help you get through law school, and it's great for cleaning out your closets, but it won't help you know your soul.

Feeling your intuitions, feeling the precious little joys in life, feeling other people's hearts, feeling your own heart is the mysterious source of endless magic that is its own truth. The degree to which you don't feel is the degree to which you're not fully alive. Goddess power is about being fully alive, about being a full, juicy human being, ripe with your own potential for love, wisdom and creation.

In the younger years, Gemini women tend to be blocked emotionally and intuitively. When that happens, the trickster aspect of the personality takes over and the tendency to game play as a source of power becomes behavior that is like breathing. Have you ever broken a thermometer and watched the mercury roll around on the floor and separate into many tiny balls? That is the effect of Mercury on the youthful personality. The behavior is detached and fragmented; the emotions are purely superficial.

When a woman hits her middle years and her feminine power has not been nurtured, her life is empty, shallow and routinized. Repetition and predictability define her life, not depth, meaning or vital emotional contact. The days turn into weeks which turn into months and the woman slowly gets older physically without getting wiser. It is common to see a Gemini woman of this ilk get caught up obsessively with exercise. It is as if by controlling her body from without, she can prevent a crumbling from within. The muscles and bones get stronger. Perhaps the ego gets stronger. However, the woman herself becomes a hollow shell. Her Goddess power is sleeping; sometimes it is snoring. And like Sleeping Beauty, it needs to be awakened if she is to be a real beauty, a beauty to the depths of herself.

In so many ways, Mercury is a dangerous planet. Like everything, its force needs to be balanced if it is to play itself out in a benevolent manner. Mercury can act very powerfully and when it becomes a tyrant, it robs a woman of her succor. It gives her a dry, canted view of life. She has only work, her routines and her dull, orderly existence. If she is in a relationship, that too becomes boring and predictable. The lethal part is if she is old enough, she will proclaim that this *is* life. Her reason will make it so. Mercury also happens to be associated with mental biases. It is the arrogance of Geminis to trust their own mental biases and call them truth, even if their own life experience is so limited that they know nothing else.

However, Mercury is also a planet of curiosity and learning. Thankfully, Gemini women have to their credit, a love of learning and an openness to new perspectives that are presented to them. What Gemini women have to realize is that there are many ways to learn, not just through the linear path of the intellect. The ways of learning through the heart and emotions are the ways of the Goddess and the path to feminine wisdom. As the Gemini woman ages, she has to open her heart so that she can hear her heart and follow its wisdom. The Gemini woman can start this process by creating rich connections with both the inner and outer world where her soul can flourish and give her the sense that the most important part of herself, that which is deep and rich and mysterious, is unfolding with time. On the other hand, the limitation of a purely Mercurial outlook will make her look at herself and others in purely superficial terms. If she doesn't know herself in deeper ways, her life will become deadened with age. There will be a sense that there is nothing interesting to look forward to. The only reason a woman born under any sign has this feeling is because she is not looking at her life in the right way.

I once had a Gemini friend who I watched die to her own feminine spirit and it was a tragic experience for me. She had once been more balanced and alive to the abundance of her feminine nature. That, combined with her high intellect and stunning sense of humor, made her company a joyous experience. But that old trickster Mercury took over her life, and her mental processes gradually edged out everything else. She achieved the highest goals she set for herself and became enormously accomplished in her chosen field. This required strenuous intellectual output over a considerable amount of time. However, gradually, her mind became cut off from her emotions and, as this happened, she could no longer perceive through a clear intuitive voice. Her head made up things that were not true. She became deluded and she completely trusted her delusions. She also became negative, angry, resentful and hostile. The day eventually came when she held no one in her heart. She alienated everyone and became a very solitary individual. As she saw it, she was victimized and this enraged her. The last time I saw her she was angry at people she didn't even know and the people she did know no longer wanted to know her. Her mind had clamped down so hard on her heart that it was like watching an animal die in a steel trap. It was impossible to talk to her. Being in her presence, listening to her litanies of betrayals and abuses, I seriously wondered if she was going insane. Her loveless life had been reduced to the pinpoint of her work. Recently I saw her name appear alongside a major intellectual accomplishment. She is highly acclaimed for her outer achievements but her soul deterioration is so terribly, terribly sad.

The dangerous thing about trusting your own limited logical Mercury mind is that it lies. And little do you know that it is laughing at you as it is lying to you. Therefore, if you give it all the power and give none to your heart and spirit, Mercury will control you and betray you. It is only a matter of time. Sometimes we may hold an opinion that is deluded or erroneous but our hearts help to straighten it out. We start to see the truth if we reflect. With our heart's help, we get beyond black and white and good and bad to a much more sophisticated, layered evaluation.

The Gemini challenge and potential is true understanding. Goddess power enables us to take more from our experiences that will enhance our life. But for this wondrous experience to happen, there has to be a slowing down of the compulsive busy activity and time must be taken for reflection. Mercury scatters energy, it encourages mental escapes: rent a movie, watch TV, make a phone call, read a magazine article, gossip, race to your next appointment. All these superficial activities take us away from the rich inner part of ourselves that needs some time and care for unfolding. These activities are Mercury's trapdoors to its secret dungeon: the trivial. However, in both Greek and Egyptian mythology, Mercury was also known as the messenger of the gods. Its highest function is to be a messenger of the god force within you—the Goddess, the seer, the wisdom, creativity and possibility of your unique horizon—that, like the ocean from the shore, always stands out there before you.

Your Dark Side

GEMINIS SUFFER FROM INSOMNIA AND ANXIETY WHICH can also lead to moodiness and depression. This can happen because Geminis' overwhelming mental energies can pull heavily on their physical vitality. There are also health problems commonly associated with this sign such as asthma, eczema, psoriasis and intestinal ailments.

The dark side of Gemini is the twin in the personality that is contracted and doesn't see far enough or feel deeply enough. The superficial mind can be quite a petty thing and in a bad moment can overtake the entire range of perception with its partial truths. Geminis tend to be critical and need to cultivate a more compassionate perspective that allows them to open up negative situations to their possibility. This is all a matter of practice, but it's a practice that must be done to avoid being victimized by the negative litanies that the lower mind loves to get into. Obsessive-compulsive thinking can cause situations to be overblown and distorted, especially when a love affair or a career performance is at stake. If not controlled, at a certain point these swarmy thoughts, like annoying freeway traffic, create their own exhaust and completely pollute the mind. Then it takes time for the cloud to disperse. However, the great thing about the changeable Gemini character is that it will pass. Geminis don't hold on to passing emotional states. They are in a constant state of flux. That's the good part. The bad part is that sometimes the fluctuations are so fast, Geminis don't learn valuable lessons from their darker states which they merely forget, toss off and bury.

When you are in turmoil, practice stopping and watching your mind. Don't identify with the contents of it. Don't *be* it. In Zen there is a wonderful term for the state of mental chaos. It is called Monkey Mind. And it is a very useful term for reining in the mind as it is spinning out of control. Simply say to yourself: That's my Monkey Mind again. Then pretend you're switching a channel on the radio to get away from the static. On this new channel hear a sound that is uniquely peaceful to you, whether that is the pounding of the surf, birds chirping at dawn or quiet forest sounds. We all have a place, preferably many places, in our mind where we would love to be if we could simply flick a switch. Let yourself imagine that place. Buy yourself some tapes of your favorite nature sounds. Nature sounds are Goddess sounds and Goddess sounds are what will bring you back into the old wise part of yourself that has peace, insight and wisdom. When you are in that place you know that the annoyances at the office are petty and you don't dwell on them. When you're in this place you're not frazzled by annoyances on the outside. You are calm, centered and fully present. When you are fully present, you see so much more that small things in life, things that you would normally rush past, start to have color and meaning.

I personally practice centering my mind because I can so easily get caught by the Monkey Mind. The Monkey Mind is contagious and devouring. It eats up the sacred, creative mind. And the more that it gobbles, the more fragmented you become. I am also an impatient person and impatient people spin out quickly if they don't work on themselves. So when I start to mentally jangle I witness my mind and label it Monkey Mind. I then stop, take a deep breath and let my annoyances disperse, reminding myself that they're meaningless and momentary. Then I bring my focus fully back to the present and make myself feel my own life force and feel gratitude for it. If you have ever been very sick in your life, it reminds you of the sacredness of your own healthy vitality. We must train ourselves not to so quickly forget that in a moment of meaningless frustration.

When the mind is slowed down it is less superficial. It is capable of perceiving sacred moments in life. These moments are always there. However, we are often too busy to see them and be moved by them. A bit of peace might be found in a brief conversation with a person whose heart is in the right place, it might be the way the light reflects on the window. It could be a flower, the snow, the wind in your face as you're walking home from work. The point is a dark day is often a dark day because your mind is dark or dull. Don't allow that. Open it up and expand it.

Our mind determines our emotions. And when the mind is rapping along on its own Monkey station, there are no positive emotions that can be had. In the extreme, this is called depression. In between is detachment and ennui. Geminis suffer a great deal from detached states. The more detached you are, the less alive you are. And often the more obsessive and compulsive you are. The mind has to be slowed down. It has to be recentered so that it works on a higher octave, a creative, inspiring octave. Diversity is a tonic to the Geminian mind-set. When the Gemini mind feels flat and unenthused it's because there are not enough stimulating people and activities in the life. Always be in the process of discovery. Never allow yourself to stop and get stuck in old patterns that no longer enliven you.

Overcoming negative mental patterns is a matter of practice and invention. Gemini women are marvelously inventive. Their problem is that they tend to not stick to things. Practice and consistency are difficult for them. But, like everything else in the Gemini makeup, that too can change!

Your Approach to Love

FAR MORE OFTEN THAN NOT, LOVE IS A SOURCE OF great confusion and distress to Gemini. Because Geminis are so headstrong and bring so many mental complications to their feelings, the love connections are usually fraught with obstacles, ambivalences, difficulties or distances of some kind. Nevertheless, Gemini women do very much value love, but because they have quite a long list of prerequisites, finding the right kind of connection is not all that easy. Gemini is also a dual sign, their unique symbol being the Twins. This doesn't simply mean a double personality, something that people so commonly associate with Geminis. On a deeper level it means the desire to complete oneself by finding the missing twin, the soul mate. When Gemini women are young, they are more interested in amusement and entertainment than love. No one nice but slightly nerdy gets a shot at showing an interesting side. Sparks have to fly for the Gemini female to even want to remember his name.

However, as Gemini women move through their thirties and beyond, they often start to believe that they have seen it all—even if what they have seen is the same sort of man over and over. There is a deeper need now to go further in terms of intimacy, to feel connected in a meaningful way. The detached playfulness of the earlier years isn't enough to sustain the soul. Now there is a need to be reached emotionally, to feel more and be more through the presence of another person. The soul is slowly starting to cry out that it wants to connect.

However, connecting is often a bit of a problem. Gemini is an air sign and air needs, above all, space and stimulating communication. And this space issue has to be dealt with correctly from the very beginning or else there will be an immediate end in sight. Some good guy who falls in love too soon and comes on too strong could make a Gemini woman ill. She can't help it. That is part of her nature that will never change. The Gemini woman needs to be stimulated and challenged. And if she isn't, if her brain is not turned on, her heart will remain cold. Some signs might find these Geminian idiosyncracies peculiar, cruel and cold. Sometimes they are. But they're also real. In the game of love, she is one woman who is not easy. She is easily suffocated emotionally and the feeling is so real that it can be felt physically. Furthermore, these feelings are just as much a discomfort to her as to any man in love with her. No matter how lonely she may be or how much she yearns to be in a loving relationship, there are only certain men that she can bear to have around her, and they consist of two types: the bad guys and the great guys.

The bad guys are an immediate comfort zone because a green light goes off in the back of her brain that says this is a harmless little situation that can eventually be escaped. The great guys are a matter of evolution. They are the life partners with whom sharing is exciting and lovers are also interesting friends. In between these two groups is a gap. And sometimes that gap is never bridged. The reason for that is the Gemini mind decides at some point that all that exists is the first group because that's all that's ever been experienced and the mind shuts down the heart. A fake bridge is created through those exciting lovers who are married or who live in foreign countries. The distance is there and it is attractive. This hurdle is an unconscious self-protection against intimacy. However, I personally feel that there is a sort of brilliance in this problem that sets up these hurdles to begin with. The brilliance is this: The Gemini woman knows that she could never love anyone she couldn't really talk to. And this basic prerequisite programmed into her genes is going to force her loving experience to move closer to evolution—or else. In between, of course, there are all those dashing callow fellows who are great fun for a few mental forays but who may mean nothing down the road. But the point is, it is a road and what to do on this road is to keep going.

Where the Goddess part of this comes in is you do something else as well. You reflect. That does not mean obsess, brood, bore yourself and others, although if you fall in love, you are sure to do some of that. It means quiet your mind. Get very still—whether you do this by sitting near a rushing stream or by listening to an uplifting piece of music. Let an intuitive voice, a pure sensibility, come through you that will guide you. Let the deepest, most ancient parts of yourself speak to yourself. They most definitely will if you silence the chatter of your superficial, rushing thoughts.

Love is the great power and all the experiences we have along the way lead up to it. They are all parts of ourselves that have to be expressed, that are leading us somewhere. Try, all alone, throwing out that very clever part of yourself that has to be in control and let that other voice come in. It will come, very slowly at first. When it comes, it will be like reading with no book, silent words coming through your mind that are wiser than you are. This wisdom will let you know what you need to know for progressing on your own special path in love. It is a path—whether you are in between relationships or actively involved in one. Just will that your mind, which is so wonderful when used to its full potential, become your source for so much wisdom and love that your heart overflows and you have to pass it on. This overflow is real human love. It's the throb of life and it's what could fill your life.

Your Power Source

I BELIEVE THAT GEMINIS ARE CAPABLE OF PRACTI-cally anything. They are possibility in motion. The source of this possibility is that the Gemini mind is curious, flexible and able to go in any direction at any given time. Geminis are also perceivers—and perceive far more than the average person.

I have Gemini friends who create moments for themselves. Giving yourself a moment—a time that you create for yourself that is very special—is pure Goddess power. It takes imagination. It also implies the willingness to be creative with your own life.

One friend would bring her favorite fruits or vegetables for snacks, put them on the front seat of her car and spend the afternoon driving in the beautiful countryside, discovering new magical places. She wrote poems about some of the wonderful things in nature she saw and how they touched her. Another took herself to the park just to draw what inspired her. Now, she is by no means an artist, but she is a person with eyes. And she loves to treat her eyes to beautiful things. On this particular day, she drew the attention of a very interesting person and during the course of their conversation, she was told by this person something very inspiring about herself. And so, she came away from this day with not only her experience of the park and her painting but with the very special experience of having meaningfully connected with another person, all of which would continue in her memory.

I have a Gemini friend who creates moments for those she cares for, and in the process, brings Goddess magic to them *and herself!* On a charcoal gray day during the last gasp of winter, she showed up at my door with a bright purple balloon trailing pink ribbons as a present to celebrate the birth of spring. Her aunt was dying of cancer and was experiencing terrible fear and physical pain. The horror of the immediate family made her overall condition worse. My friend visited her every day with a smile on her face. She made her laugh because she knew that was exactly what she needed. She bought her bright colored dresses she was able to find in consignment shops. Every day, before she went to work, she called her to ask what special food she needed for her soul and then, having gotten up extra early, she cooked it and brought it to her. Telling me of these moments, my friend glowed. I looked at her with a mixture of awe and wonder. "How are you doing this?" I asked her. "How are you not sucked up by the terrible sadness?" She replied that she knew that her aunt needed light and giving that to her gave them both something so positive and worthwhile that *that* was what she focused on. What a divine use of Gemini detachment. How often people focus on the negative aspect of Gemini detachment. But there can be a very positive use as well. You don't become someone else's pain. Instead you address their life. Gemini can detach *through* love and not just *from* love. And certainly that is the power of the Goddess.

The challenge of the Gemini soul is to be conscious, conscious of the life and joy and spirit in everything. The way that Gemini transcends her own tendency to be superficial is through developing a higher quality of thinking that is based on meditating on the meaning of things—and trusting that there is a meaning, even if it can't be uncovered in the moment. Sometimes that meaning comes from an emotion that rises to the surface when you least expect it. But whatever it is, it is always important to be able to go deeper to see patterns, to be open to mysteries, and to be willing to be wrong about preconceived notions.

A conscious mind also asks the right questions. What is this person feeling? How can I help? How can I see and feel more? What is the meaning of this experience? What can I learn here? These are some questions that are necessary to think about when one holds consciousness as a value.

The course of a day is completely different in a mind that is conscious versus a mind that is unconscious. A conscious person is capable of experiencing so much more that the experience of life itself can be a wondrous adventure. Geminis need wonder. They are also capable of perceiving and receiving wonder as it unfolds around them. And most of all, they are capable of creating wondrous experiences. Creating wonder for ourselves and others doesn't cost anything. It is a matter of valuing possibility—in all things, at all times—and being able to stretch toward that. That is the unique Geminian Goddess power. Use it, share it, think about it and talk about it. Little by little the world will change all around you.

CANCER
(June 22–July 23)

Your Essential Self

HIGHLY EMOTIONAL AND DEEPLY SENTIMENTAL, THE Cancer woman is perhaps the most vulnerable of all the signs. Ruled by the moon, the planet which is associated with the unconscious as well as with the Goddess, the archtypal feminine principle, she is both feminine and moody. She is also intuitive and sensitive, picking up subtleties that pass others by. Sometimes she is too sensitive and takes things too personally. Subjectivity can be a problem in this sign that is also known for the protective shell it can wear.

The Cancer woman has an emotional life that is very demanding. Her need for emotional intimacy as well as emotional security is great. Therefore, she places enormous importance on having a love relationship which leads to marriage and a family. Children are very important to her, just as emotional security is a necessity for her emotional well-being.

There are times when she can be very difficult:

moody, changeable, demanding, draining, clingy. At other times she can be loving, nurturing, sensitive, sweet and self-sacrificing, giving of herself on many levels, a sympathetic soul who understands and is willing to share another's pain.

The hardest things for a Cancer woman to learn or accept are emotional boundaries. Letting go is not her forte. At times she can clutch too hard and rein in too close. She can be a devoted mother and wife but has difficulty backing off and allowing those she loves the space or alone time that they may require. Too much emotional centering in others can put her totally off center, making her dependent and robbing her of her power.

Maintaining a delicate balance between caring for herself and others is a challenge for this woman. She can also extend this problem to her career by overly extending herself and not knowing when enough is enough. This can make her the boss from hell, the mother who is the martyr and the wife or lover who is the victim. All of these situations can come about because she can't easily say to herself or others, "Enough! No more!"

The moon is a most mysterious planet. In mythology, moon goddesses are both creative and destructive. They are givers of life and power and they are also devouring and consume power. Cancer women carry these archaic paradoxes around in their psyches. No wonder, at times they feel a primal need for emotional security. No wonder, on occasion, they get moody and cranky. To feel so much, even in the most mundane situations is not easy.

At times the mind and heart are like a mysterious heavy weight that defies rationality. Moods come and go like the tides. Like the phases of the moon, they pass into something else and sink down into the depths of the unconscious. Through it all, the experience of love sustains the soul and lights the way. The Cancer woman finds meaning in those intimate moments when she is connected to her own life force through her connection to those she loves.

Your Dark Side

THE JUNGIAN ANALYST JUNE SINGER SAYS OF THE mythological Great Mother, the symbol for the power of the unconscious, "She is the terrible female whose awesome power looms over the child—boy or girl— she knows all there is to know and from her everything must be learned—she metes out punishment or affection according to her own unfathomable laws."

When she says "she knows all there is to know," she is referring symbolically to the power of the unconscious, the power of the purely intuitive and nonrational. The punishment, of course, are the moods and fears or painful emotional states that mysteriously come and go in a Cancer. The Great Mother is symbolically the power of lunar consciousness, the nonrational sphere of the moon.

As a Cancer, a creature of the moon, a woman will know darkness and emotional fluctuations. And those who live with her know it too. Sometimes it is as if some of her psychic energy has leaked out and her enthusiasm for life is on hold. She has to live with a self that she doesn't always understand, the mysterious lunar consciousness—which is her unconscious rising through her conscious day-to-day life. When this happens, her psyche passes into the dark of the moon. And what is particularly difficult is that she is living in a solar world where rationality rules. Therefore, at such times she can feel out of sync—not only with herself but with the whole world.

At such times, when possible, retreat and withdrawal are necessary. If the Cancer woman doesn't understand herself, she must understand her process, that her psyche changes like the phases of the moon. When it goes into a dark phase, and she feels bored or deadened or drained or melancholy, it is not that nothing is happening in her life. Usually, a great deal is happening but it is occurring underneath the surface, in her unconscious. Psychic energy, which is creative energy, is being rerouted there and stored up.

This is an important time which a Cancer woman should treat as sacred and in which she should nurture her psyche as she would nurture a newborn infant. Granted, she may have to go to work and can't drop all of her mundane responsibilities and withdraw. However, she can still find some time in the day for herself—if she tries. And she should use that time to be very quiet, to contemplate or write in a journal and let her unconscious speak to her. This could be the time when she creates her very best poetry and it will be poetry that is saying something important to her.

This is a psychic time and a creative time. In primitive tribes women always withdrew once a month when they got their period. However, although this withdrawal had a cultural base, it had then and still has a psychological value. In these times, the Cancer woman must do things or be around things that represent the feminine. For instance, nature is feminine. A walk in the woods or the park, lying in the sun, or visiting an aquarium could help put her in touch with her own deep nature. Also, some solitary creative time for writing poetry, reading something inspirational, painting one's feelings, is also important. The significant point is that it is possible to reach new levels of oneself by treating this time as sacred and facilitating the mood, encouraging it to speak to you. This dark period can be a highly fertile period, a time to reach a new level of richness in one's personal spirituality and creativity. Creativity is godly. It is the domain of the Goddess. When we appeal to the Goddess within ourselves, we are starting to unleash our own feminine power which is greater meaning and understanding based on intuition and wisdom. The richer the meaning of one's life, the greater the life, the greater the range of oneself.

The Goddess was also the deity of fertility, the fertility not only of the earth but of one's consciousness—which is part of the great creative power of the universe. So, let the darkness bring you past the petty and purely personal to the divine mystery of yourself. Allow yourself to be renewed through it so that the light of the full moon will shine through your consciousness and you will be ever renewed.

Your Approach to Love

ROMANTIC, SENTIMENTAL, SENSUAL AND VERY EMOtional, the Cancer woman believes in the power of love. Love is her *raison d'etre*. Lovelessness is like a slow, sweeping depression that leaves her melancholy and lifeless.

Sailing into romantic situations with her heart rather

than her head, the Cancer woman often tends to see what she would like to see rather than the true picture. Often disappointed and disillusioned when her projected hero turns into a soulless cad, she can't get back on her feet as quickly as some of her astrological sisters. Love is serious business for the Cancer woman. It must be lasting and it must satisfy the romantic, sensual part of her personality. A marriage that is lifeless can eat away at her. It might very well be worse than no relationship at all, for it pushes her back on herself in the worst way. It makes her sad and it fills her with longing.

While some signs put more importance on materialism, accomplishment, conquest or sex only for the sake of sex, the Cancer woman looks for meaning in love. This meaning comes first and is found not only through romantic love but also through home, children and family.

However, the road to attaining this cherished ideal can often be rocky, perhaps because it sometimes means so much. Another reason is that the Cancer woman does not look before she leaps and sometimes leaps into the arms of a villain whose passion appeals to her need for great romantic love. Although highly intuitive, the Cancer woman is not good at reading the signs of danger because basically she wants to believe the best. Even if a situation is ostensibly bad, it is not in her nature to walk away. It is her emotional style to assume it will get better.

And so, she has been known to hold on to something that no longer serves her well, as well as to something that perhaps didn't even exist in the first place in the way that her idealistic self thought it existed. While all women love to be swept away by a romantic appeal to their feelings, the Cancer woman leads the group.

Highly sentimental and emotionally attached to beautiful memories, the woman born under this sign will not easily give up the ship once it is sinking or perhaps has already sunk. She firmly believes in forever and if she can have her way, she'll will it with all her heart.

Cancers have often been accused of being emotionally masochistic. However, I think that Cancerian emotional behavior is much more complex than that. It is a combination of emotional need, wishful thinking and fear of a future alone. All of this combined causes her to hold on like the crab pinching its claws.

As the Cancer woman develops and comes more in touch with her power as an individual, she will learn to value her own life as much as a "secure" relationship. She will start to live through her own psychic, intuitive, creative powers and trust them with equal sanctity as she does her partnership. Consequently, she will come to the right partnership as someone striving to be whole rather than someone seeking to escape a little lonely self.

There is much for the Cancer woman to learn from the lessons of love. Ideally, these lessons will bring her to a deeper, richer relationship with herself that will keep growing and evolving. When she turns inward in the right way through meditation, contemplation, creativity and spiritual pursuits—making her life a sacred act of love to herself, she will likewise become more powerful in love—with both her partner and her children. She will start to live from her Source—the ancient, archtypal wisdom and beauty of the Goddess—and her wounds will be healed by the little piece of heaven in her heart.

Your Power Source

THE GREAT POWER OF THE CANCER WOMAN IS THE ability to create and care for life. Her creativity and capability for love is boundless, as is her ability to create through her imagination.

The most obvious creativity associated with this sign is motherhood. It is very rare to ever encounter a Cancer woman who is indifferent to becoming a mother. Pregnancy, childbirth and motherhood have deep spiritual meaning for her. The love that comes from an intimate, caring relationship with her children is a profoundly emotional experience. For many Cancer women it can be even more powerful than their relationship with their husband, which will have its ups and downs and periods of noncommunication.

At any rate, the experience of being a mother has a primordial value for the Cancer woman. She is a very internal person and she comes to meet life from a place deep within her, just as from a place deep within her springs life. Therefore, the child has a psychic, spiritual bearing on her own relationship to herself. It is not so much life that comes from her but life that is a mysterious part of her.

Nevertheless, physical motherhood is by no means her only form of creativity. Her imagination and extraordinary sensitivity as well as her keen intuition make her a natural in all forms of artistic expression. As I have already said, Cancer is ruled by the moon, the symbol of psychic as well as physical fertility. It is also the planet associated with the mysteries and fluctuations of consciousness that can give forth wisdom, deeper emotional understanding and creativity. The wonderful novelist Louise Erdrich is a great example of a Cancer woman who honors the sacredness of giving birth on all levels. In both her poetry, "Baptism of Desire," and her nonfiction, *The Blue Jay's Dance,* she shows the mysterious interweaving of the various levels of creativity available to a woman, from giving birth to a child to the process of writing. In her poem, "The Ritual," her words, "Soon, I say to the unborn one turning beneath the heart of the sleeping woman, you will break from me and be recognized," apply to the primordial spirit of creativity within the sleeping consciousness of woman as well as to the anticipation of the birth of a child.

There is also great healing ability in the Cancer woman's emotions at their fullest potential. The challenge of all of us is to rise above the merely personal, the littleness of our lives that keeps us insulated on a lower level of consciousness. When the Cancer woman is able to extend beyond the merely personal, when she is able to show compassion and love for those around her and when she is able to derive personal meaning from that, she carries a great deal of archetypal feminine power, the power to heal the heart, the mind, the body and the spirit.

A great Cancer woman who is an example of this power is Elizabeth Kubler-Ross. A doctor who is a pioneer in the field of death and dying, she has over the years, worked with thousands of people, helping them make the transition and find meaning in the process. A true heroine in every sense of the word, she has reached beyond her own family and personal concerns to bring her intelligence, sensitivity, compassion and insight to this subject and her fellow human beings. Through love and true Cancerian determination, she has been a healing force who has made herself heard far and wide. Even as an older woman in her seventies who had suffered a stroke, she was busy setting up an AIDS hospice on the farm where she lived—with her own money that she received from lectures. Both this farm and her previous farm were burned down because ignorant people did not appreciate her work. Elizabeth lost everything. All the animals died in this man-made fire. This would be enough to devastate another person. However, her indomitable Cancerian tenacity kept her going and she overcame it all.

Cancerian love is a great healing power. It is the gift of the Goddess, the greatness of the soul coming to shine among human beings to enable them to rise above. Cancerian sensitivity, understanding and compassion can create a great bridge to the hearts of others, giving them a sense of meaning and possibility they might not have otherwise. When a Cancer woman is able to give to herself in meaningful ways, she also has more power to give to others and her life comes to be defined by the light in her heart.

LEO
(July 24–August 23)

Your Essential Self

LEO IS THE ASTROLOGICAL SIGN ASSOCIATED WITH SELF. From an early age, Leo females have a strong self-awareness. In their waking dreams, their deepest desire is to see their exalted reflection in the outside world. The Leo dream is the dream of perfection. The fantasy is to become a myth in the making, a woman who is a blinding presence who is recognized, respected and worshipped for her light.

Recognition and accomplishment are extremely important to the Leo woman. She is always judging herself and the standard is based on personal achievement. However, being a restless, impatient sort she doesn't satisfy her own towering standards for very long. She has to keep proving herself to herself. And this involves exceeding herself time and time again.

Leos want to be like the blazing summer sun at high noon. Anything less is seen by Leos as embarrassing and mediocre. This attitude is at the base of all that infamous Leonian ambition. While other signs may strive because of dollar signs dancing in the back of their brains, the Leo thrust is for self-definition through excellence.

When everything works according to plan, this picture is perfect. However, when there are a lot of bumps or blank spaces along the way, this attitude can be truly crazy making. On the negative end, Leo women can get blocked before they've even done anything because of their sickening fear of failure. When those terrifying words "what if" creep into the mind and take over, slowly the picture of the goal is supplanted by the possibility of what might happen if the performance doesn't meet the necessary optimum standards. This strain on the ego of always having to be perfect or of having to accomplish more and more, is like trying to have a great time traveling when you're carrying all your luggage on your back. It's not much fun but more to the point, you're really not going to go very far.

The great irony of this situation is that when Leos are seen for their accomplishments, the light can be so radiant that people assume that they really didn't have to work to get there. People often think of archetypal Leos as just being born blinding and having nothing more to do than show up. This is certainly not the case. Leo women toil hard and long to attain their dreams. And when they're not actually working, they're planning things out in their head. They just don't talk about everything they're doing because they're usually doing so much and they're thinking so far ahead.

One thing that Leo women have to be careful of is overkill. Another is the motive behind their involvements. If they are doing what they are doing because they genuinely love it, then that is a healthy route to their own happiness. However, if they are taking on their projects in an effort to prove or maintain their worth, they are heading for trouble. A Leo woman has to love herself regardless of her achievements, not because of them. When the self-value is so contingent on meeting standards of externals, then one is not living authentically. One is living one's life through a veil of fear. And this fear can shut down the ability to fully express rich, exciting talents.

Leo is also the sign associated with the fifth house of children. Within the Leo woman is a wonderful, breathless child blowing out the candles at her own birthday party. This child within is playful and mischievous. It is full of expectation and loves fairy tales. The child within sees clearly that life should be fun. It demands dazzle and peak experiences. She also has the ability to make the mundane magical. The Leo woman has a natural love of life which she generously bestows on everything and everyone important to her. It is the source of her enthusiasm and the key to her own sense of possibility. With this infectious spirit she can inspire and heal others' spirits.

This golden spirit enables her to create from life, to have a large view that encompasses far-reaching possibilities. It is the sort of mind that can create its own miracles because it is linked so deeply to the heart. The Leo woman's heart is the key to her divinity. When her heart is in its natural place and not clouded by fear or depression or overshadowed by ego needs, she brings a sense of abundance to everything she focuses on. Is it a wonder that she can be so much fun? The Leo woman believes in joy and instinctively knows the healing nature of beauty. She knows that beauty is a tonic for the soul. Her love and her light is the most wholesome Goddess energy. Regardless of the darkness that may be part of her life journey, her self will always search for the light. When she is able to actually live it in her own authentic way, it will define her and she will light the way for others.

Your Dark Side

I ALWAYS THINK OF THE DARK SIDE OF LEO AS THE blackened sun. Leo women who experience darkness in their souls are usually quiet about it. This isn't only because their pride doesn't want the world to know that they're down. It is also because to talk about the darkness is to call attention to it, and deep inside, there is a part of the Leo woman who wants to snuff her pain and prays for it to lift like the sort of summer thunderstorm that leaves a rainbow.

However, there is value in a mood or depression. It makes us slow down and reflect. It throws us back on our inner world and creates a break with the outside world. There is also a value to the bad times. They have meaning. They are there for a purpose. There is something important to learn about ourselves from them. If we have enough courage and insight we can be transformed by them. And that means attaining a deeper, wiser self that can encompass both darkness and light.

Sometimes the darkness requires that we let go and surrender to something we don't even understand. There is a power to this. It's in knowing you *can* let go and let things be and that everything will turn out as it should. This might be the most difficult lesson a Leo woman can ever learn in her entire life because there is a tape in her head that says she must be in control. A Leo woman who does not feel in control of herself is in a very dangerous place—she fears she will fail or betray herself. This brittle attitude can be very self-sabotaging. Furthermore, it lends itself to a self-fulfilling prophecy. Worry and fear feed into her soul and they need to be replaced with faith.

A perfectionist about everything she seriously aims to accomplish, the Leo woman sets herself up for a great deal of anxiety and tension. The anxiety is not necessarily always conscious. It may be unconscious and fuel her with a compulsive energy. However, at a certain point, if she is operating from her compulsions instead of her conscious awareness, this anxiety will at some point bleed through into the conscious mind, creating more anxiety and a sense of dread. A Leo woman caught in the throes of this kind of anxiety may attribute it to any number of causes: her oncoming period, money problems, insecurity over her lover. And some of her real-life problems may very well be making their generous contribution. However, if she is also driving herself hard by intransigent standards of excellence which is emblematic of her character, she is also setting up a powerful dichotomy to work against herself. If she achieves her vision of her goal, she gets only a temporary high like an addictive drug. If she fails, she feels humiliated. No one could ever be harder on the Leo woman than she is on herself. And the irony is that this little setup she has created for herself in her mind will never bring her the kind of inner power she so longs for. It can't. It is self-punishing not self-affirming. And in order to continue smiling as she plays this game, she has to become a better and better actress.

The successful route to real self-worth requires that you abandon this program and supplant it with love. Love who you are regardless of your achievements. Love what you do so much that you have to do it, regardless of the outcome. Start every day with positive, enthusiastic self-talk. You'll know when you're getting the right results: You start to relax. Something deep inside you starts to trust. When things go against you, you no longer feel like a pretzel that's been overbaked. Your mind starts to slow down so there's more clarity and less emotional static. Now you are starting to operate from your Goddess power, not your mind's distorted cues from your environment.

To do the most with this precious life of which you are the recipient, you have to persist in affirming yourself to yourself, *especially* when things don't go your way. This means in front of the mirror in the morning (as corny as it may sound) and in the quiet of your bed before you go to sleep. During the day, create your own secret time-outs when you give yourself the kind of heartfelt encouragement you would bestow upon a friend you admire. Don't take yourself or your gifts for granted in any way. Be grateful for all the wonderful qualities with which you came into this world.

On a very bad day, slow down, take a break, switch gears and take it all one step at a time. Losing your temper is only going to bring you to an even lower level. Learn how to plod through your fear. Outwalk it. Outthink it. Outtalk it. And most of all, go for the meaning in those things that make you most upset.

Gain an awareness from them that gives your perspectives dimension.

If you are in a job you hate, think about what *would* give you the sense of meaning that would make you feel more alive. Go for meaning. Don't confine yourself to status—unless you are prepared to play with it for a while and not let it own you. It's all wonderful and interesting when you get creative with your decisions. It is only the Leo sense of drama that makes you fear doom. But doom is nothing more than your mental attitude. And you are a miracle in the making. You will know that for yourself when you step out of yourself and see your own light. It is always there, even if you don't feel it. However, when you become aware of it, you will know the depth of your own Goddess power and it will sustain you. When you come to trust it, when it is so strong there is no place left inside for self-invented fear, with each breath you will flow into what you should be doing for the love of your life. You will then be acutely conscious that that is all the power you will ever need.

Your Approach to Love

THE PART OF THE BODY ASSOCIATED WITH LEO IS THE heart. Leo women love to be touched through their heart. They also love to be in love and can be strongly swayed by their emotions.

For Leo, love is like a theatrical event. Leo women lend to it their natural sense of largesse which includes their sense of extravagance and glamour. Leo women see themselves as highly selective in the sort of lover they would gravitate toward. However, they can also be blinded by someone inferior who has a great deal of charm, magic, whimsy, razzle-dazzle and not a whole lot of character.

When madly in love, the Leo woman tends to mythologize her experience and her lover. It is as if she is living out some grand scheme of fate destined only for those capable of such grandness. In psychology, such grandiose perspectives are called inflationary attitudes and they are usually a precursor to the fall. Ultimately, of course, this does happen. However, in the meantime, the Leo woman has a wonderful time projecting onto her lover a towering ideal which is some aspect of herself not fully owned or authentically realized.

Restless and needing drama and excitement, Leo women often tend to prefer glamorous, romantic events to too many quiet nights at home. Archtypal Leos can't take too much nitty-gritty, boring, real-world stuff. The MGM production is far more their taste: flourish and dash and glamour and highly flattering romantic glow. Like everything else that's important to Leo, being in love must be like a flood-light that makes even the dusty little corners of their lives glow.

It might be said that Leo women are far more in love with the larger-than-life experience of love than with the actual person. When madly in love, they don't see the person and in fact do more than a little to invent him, extend him and help him along to become a superlative. When that day comes that the imperfect person emerges to the cruel light of day, the Leo woman is capable of running quite cold. She is not someone to hang on forever or pine away for years. Even if it is very painful, once she sees that the situation is no good for her, she will eliminate it and make herself live with her decision. This is because what the Leo woman values even more than love is her individuality and her survival. If this is seriously at risk, the relationship has to go.

When she becomes more mature and has lived through more of herself, the Leo woman will not have the same need to project that she had when she was restless and seeking excitement. It is possible, now that she has grown, for her to attract a truly rich connection based on soul qualities of deep communication, mutual respect and the sort of relating that is vital and generative. Now she has the potential to really live through the mystery of her heart, to really be touched by the mystery of love which is powerful and transformative. Here she reaches a new level of aliveness as she is touched by the power of what a human love connection can be. Of course, she will embrace this newly found superlative, but this time it is one that won't disappoint her.

Your Power Source

LEO WOMEN ARE INTENSELY ALIVE, THEY EXUDE AN emotional vitality that has its own life force. The powerful fire energy that bubbles up through them is magnetic and arresting. It is the fuel for their exuberance and their childlike enthusiasm.

On the highest level, Leo is the sign of spirit, the divine spark that is the light of every soul. It is spirit that makes them yearn to transcend their limitations. It is the Leo heart that can open up like a flower to make others feel a deep, immediate connection.

The spirit and the heart together make for a rich soulful quality of life and a love of life. Leo women show love for their life through how they dress, how they decorate, how they create and how they play.

This is a highly creative sign that is sensitive to light and color. One Leo woman I know, who always looks perfect, wears only colors in the gold family which compliments her own coloring. Gold is also the color of Leo. With her extraordinary joie de vivre and magnanimous heart, she always looks like a resplendent golden Goddess. This woman, who is a whirlwind of energy and excitement about so many things, is like a child at Christmas. I remember one afternoon I spent with her in which she was talking about her life. She sighed and said, "I love it all! I just love it all!"

Such is the glittering, Goddess-given spirit of Leo. It bursts forth like lightning, or it can be quiet and heartfelt. But it is always so contagious and moving that it inspires. At her best, a Leo woman can inspire others to exceed themselves and love themselves. There is something about her heartfelt sincerity that is so convincing. And, of course, she loves to inspire. It is her nature, a nature that cannot be contained, a nature that must overflow and radiate outward in a stream of positive energy.

It is part of her generous, expansive nature that loves to give and loves to make an uplifting difference in the lives of others, especially those she loves. She is a loyal friend and lover and to all her relationships she brings her imagination, her generosity and her sense of magic. Instinctively, she knows how to create exciting moments. She also knows how to conjure captivating settings that influence a mood.

Leo women love to make a difference. They care,

deep in their hearts, about the quality of life. That is why they place such an emphasis on beauty in the surroundings. They want their surroundings to be a reminder of all the beauty that is in life. They want to dwell on this beauty. Being highly idealistic, they tend to go for the beauty in people, blocking out the character flaws. I have a Leo friend who is forever telling me in the most excited way about some new person she has met who I must meet. Immediately, I feel myself getting caught up and transported by her view of all these people who sound so wonderful. When I'm hearing all this, it doesn't matter to me what these people are really like. What matters is that I want to share in the contagious enthusiasm that she feels.

Leo women communicate pleasure like no other sign. They expect pleasure and they receive it from a million things. Meeting a wonderful person is, of course, at the top of the list. However, there are so many things, both large and small, that delight them in the most spontaneous way. So much has been written about the Leonine penchant for extravagance. However, Leo women are most deeply moved by someone's thought, which costs nothing. They are most appreciative of a walk in the woods, a flower, the way the sun dapples a lawn on a summer afternoon and they can be like children with the love and beauty they hold in their hearts. The most sophisticated Leo woman loves to read fairy tales, skip through an open field and can plop down and color in a coloring book with a bunch of children. She loves to create. She loves to paint, write poetry, reflect in a journal. She also loves to dance. But she can be equally creative with cooking, with setting a beautiful candlelit table, or with giving a party that is imaginative and unique. All creative acts are the domain of the Goddess. At her most inspired, the Leo woman can put it all together and make theater, theater in the metaphorical sense where everything is treated with such impeccable care that its power is spellbinding. The Leo woman especially knows how to captivate because she herself is so easily transported by beauty and kindness. Her special power is to spread beauty and kindness all around her like a light. Her Goddess message is, "Love it! Love it *all* and share it with those you love."

VIRGO
(August 24–September 23)

Your Essential Self

THE VIRGO WOMAN IS LED THROUGH LIFE BY HER head. However, it is not the "flying through space" sort of head of the Aquarius woman or the idealistic "pie in the sky" sort of head of the Leo. It is a thoughtful, discriminating, prudent head that is connected to a body with two feet firmly planted on earth going somewhere. Virgo women are practical thinkers prepared to take some sort of purposeful action. They like to make complicated things simple by looking at them with the proper focus. And Virgos also like to be fully prepared for any chaos that might potentially come along.

The symbol associated with Virgo is the virgin. However, virgin did not originally mean what it does today. Its primal meaning is being self-contained and mistress of oneself. There is a self-containment about the Virgo woman. It can be seen in the cool demeanor she projects, a demeanor that can often be mistaken for coldness and indifference. In truth, it is simple reserve. Virgo women are a bit slow to get to know. It is not their style to spontaneously jump in and tell you their entire life story during a first meeting, nor is it their style to become friends in five minutes. Virgo women respond at their own pace. They extend outward in a slow, quiet and tentative way and can be a little shy about taking the first step.

Cool, capable, efficient and in for life once they've decided you're worthwhile, Virgos are loyal, long-lasting friends who love to help those they care about. In the realm of professional caring, they make excellent nurses, doctors, psychologists and astrologers.

Virgo is the sign of health. So often one finds those born under this sign concerned with diet, nutrition and all kinds of health practices and alternative preventative health regimes. Virgo is also an analytical sign that thinks things through, carefully assimilating all the details to understand all the many interrelated parts of the picture. A deliberating, conservative thinker rather than a bold, impassioned risk taker, the Virgo woman accomplishes her goals at a sure, steady pace. Control, safety and security are considerations at all times. The Virgo woman needs to know where she stands and have a sense of where she's going. And this is true in every aspect of her life—from work to love.

Virgo women love to learn and have a great respect for knowledge. There are some who come off as "know-it-alls" as a compensation for other insecurities. However, in general, she follows through on what she has learned and makes practical use of her knowledge. This sort of Virgo woman can be very interesting to talk to because she is always working things through and coming to new levels of awareness.

Virgo women have delicate nervous systems and are prone to worry. They can suffer physically from imposing pressures and difficult people. Consequently, they need a bit of solitude and meaningful quiet time to recuperate from the harsh effects of the world at large. A cup of tea, a good book, some restful music and the presence of a favorite animal is wonderful therapy. Virgo is the sign of small animals, so it's not uncommon to find a couple cats holding court in their homes. Because cats are so relaxed and self-assured and certainly worry about nothing, their presence can have quite a healing effect on this sign.

Although they have a wonderful, intelligent sense of humor, Virgo women are basically serious and take everything close to them seriously—sometimes too seriously for their own good. Prone to psychosomatic disorders, skin eruptions, headaches, stomach problems and emotional fatigue, their bodies take the brunt of what their minds can't stomach. Virgo women are not good at letting things go and quickly moving on. They often hold on too long to the wrong things.

Because this is a sign ruled by Mercury, the planet of thinking and analyzing, the Virgo woman is more comfortable in this realm than in her emotions. She needs to deal with conflicts and problems in her own way and in her own time. She also can't be rushed by outside influences to make any moves or come to any important decisions. Often a Virgo does take so long to find her own voice that tension builds up and undermines her.

The greatest challenge of the Virgo woman is to look at the things that she considers so powerful or menacing and see the power she is investing in them. It is a power she is taking away from herself. It is *her* power that she is misappropriating. When she starts to realize this and consciously work on it, as I have seen some Virgo women do, she is on the path to her own virginal self, her own powerful self-containment, and from this path new power and wisdom will continue to unfold for her.

Your Dark Side

THERE IS A FAIR AMOUNT OF FEAR IN THIS SIGN—FEAR of the worst that can happen, along with a tendency to dwell on the negativities of the past and treat them as if they were tied to a future fate. Virgo women can worry excessively about so many things that it seriously slows them down. In the worst-case scenario, this preoccupation can incapacitate them, keeping them locked into place, unable to move forward in the right way.

There can be a bit of a martyr in the Virgo woman. This she plays out through letting others take advantage and then being angry and resentful afterward. This kind of resentment can really build up, pollute the mind, and eventually, the body. Virgo women need to be firm about their boundaries and think of the big picture—what their agonized silence will cost them down the road. They should also not put themselves in situations in which they are giving more than they can afford to. Because their nervous system is so sensitive, they have to be self-protective.

A fundamental problem this sign can have is not seeing the forest for the trees. Virgo women can have a very small view of things that can completely sabotage their perception of what's really important. Petty attitudes, grudge-bearing and absorption with details to the exclusion of the big picture are dark Virgo traits. This is fear based behavior. This kind of grocery list thinking ensures a certain secure place in the small scheme of things. And that place is the trap of growing old in utter meaninglessness, a meaninglessness that is death for the spirit and the soul.

The negative Virgo woman can be very compulsive about her meaningless routines and details. They give her a false sense of control that can be habit-forming. This can be a very obsessive sign—about the most nonessential things. Virgo women often have an obsessive need for order which controls them to the exclusion of finding meaning and intrinsic value in their acts.

Virgo can also be too subjective, small-minded and judgmental, concerned only with her view of right and wrong and having no insight into the complex emotional circumstances that have gone into creating a very human situation. Here she can be incredibly cut off from the full range of her own humanity. And when she is, she is also completely divorced from her Goddess power.

There can be a really cold, unreachable quality in this kind of Virgo woman who is such a victim of her own attitudes. Her littleness begets littleness and it can come to define her entire life. The saddest thing in a human being's life is not the tragedies—which have a transforming value—but the deadness in life that some people embrace and call life. When the mind has closed in on itself, as it can with Virgo, no light can enter. The mind becomes like a cave with no reflections. However, when we are open, we are also open to reflect others and to be reflected. This is one important way we can learn and grow. Therefore, it is so important to struggle beyond the tip of the nose to the potential in people and the truth that is all around you. When you do, life speaks to you in many ways—through people, through metaphor and increasingly through your own intuition. When this richness starts to supercede obsessive attention to meaningless details, compulsive talking that communicates nothing significant and compulsive eating or working as a substitute for emptiness, there is increasingly color and energy in life. The greatest gift a Virgo woman can give herself is the gift of her own life. Here I offer a quote from an Indian sage, Satish Kumar, "We are all life longing for itself. The image of the dancing Shiva in Indian temples is of all existence in a continuous dance. We create our own techniques of dancing; the challenge is to see how finely we can dance. That is the purpose of life."

Your Approach to Love

IN EVERYTHING SHE DOES THE VIRGO WOMAN IS SERIous. Her experience of love is no different.

Initially she may be slow in getting involved. For one, she is a finely tuned mixture of diffident, cautious and critical. She is also highly self-protective and afraid of getting hurt. The Virgo woman does not bounce back easily from heartaches or betrayal. Indeed, she can become consumed by hurt, anger and bitterness and it can affect her for the rest of her life. One thing is certain—once she has been seriously burned by a situation she will be very, very slow to jump back into the fire again. As a matter of fact, her strong sense of self-protectedness will see to it that the next time she will have much more control.

There are Virgo women, who, after a couple of bad experiences, turn cold and cynical, completely cutting themselves off from the prospect of love. In the Tarot, Virgo is associated with the Major Arcana card, the Hermit and sometimes Virgo needs to withdraw from the world at large in order to heal its emotional and psychological wounds.

A Virgo woman is never one to throw caution to the wind like her fire sign sisters. At all times she must feel that she knows where she stands as well as where she is going. Therefore, she tends to shy away from wild, flashy types and gravitates toward men who make her feel secure.

However, there are always exceptions. Occasionally a man will come along who reflects her irrational shadow side and often when this happens she doesn't have the time to know what hit her. The reasonable part of her might try to fight it or at least mildly protest. Often this resistance gives more power to the enchantment resulting in obsession. However, at some point reason will usually regain its hold and then it is amazing to see how quickly love can turn into hate.

The Virgo woman fares best with a kind, stable man she can talk to like a friend. It is even better if she respects his mind and is stimulated by it. Trust is also crucially important to her. When she feels she can trust, she will joyfully commit herself without losing herself. Unlike certain women of other signs who can lose their identity in a relationship, the Virgo woman always keeps a little of herself in reserve. She may be intensely involved in some study that occupies some of her time. She may be involved with crafts or painting. Most definitely, she will need reading time and personal improvement time in which she might write in a journal or dedicate herself to some writing project. At any rate, she knows how to make good use of her alone time and it is something that is very important to her.

In this, Virgo has much to pass on to some of her astrological sisters. The Virgo woman successfully maintains that delicate line between loving another and caring for herself. This is a powerful Goddess attitude. To care for one's own physical and spiritual existence as much as one cares for another is something many women need to learn. The Virgo woman values her own mind and spirit enough not to lose it. She also knows that losing it is not a requirement for love. Indeed, that sort of love is merely an excuse for losing a self that is not properly valued. In love as in everything else, the Virgo woman has values that define her and determine a great deal of her fate. The very foundation of her attitude is a sense of responsibility that completely affirms her.

Your Power Source

AT HER BEST, THERE IS A CAPACITY TO CARE IN THE Virgo woman which can be healing and transformative. The combination of her groundedness and ability to act from a vision of what could be—beyond the disease, the neurosis, the social limitation—can make her a powerful doctor, healer, psychotherapist, midwife, social worker or veterinarian. She is also a patient, enduring person who can work successfully in the background. She does not have to be in the front lines or in the limelight soaking up all the glory. She finds meaning in serving and serving well.

The evolved Virgo woman is serious, conscientious, intellectually inquisitive and completely committed to anything she takes on. She is invaluable in the helping professions and committed to her ideal of justice. The Virgo woman is most powerful when her heart is also present. Her kindness, commitment and desire to be of help and to effect positive change put her ahead of many of her astrological sisters who can't stretch far enough to contribute quite so much.

When positive, the Virgo woman is not so much interested in perfection for the sake of perfection as she is in improvement and a better way of life. She is always reading, studying and seeking new ways of finding meaning in the puzzle of life. Taking courses, attending lectures and studying new things—especially in the areas of psychology, health and metaphysics—she is always evaluating possibilities. Because her analytical ability is so keen, she makes a wonderful astrologer or Jungian analyst. And because she keeps pushing herself along in the search for greater truths, she makes a stimulating conversationalist as well as a great group facilitator or lecturer.

The key to the wonderful Virgo woman is that she keeps going—despite her fears, frustrations, conflicts, menacing challenges and personal tragedies. Relentlessly, she keeps digging for meaning through it all. And in the process, she keeps expanding herself and her own sense of possibility.

Her diligence, persistence and sheer love of learning make her a woman many women could learn from. The purity of the vision she holds so close to her heart makes her an impressive voice of intelligence and integrity, while her trenchant insights set her apart from those who are merely intellectual. The powerful Virgo woman has the ability to synthesize all of her information and gain new meaning in the process. With her penetrating mind, she can contribute much to the world.

The powerful Virgo woman is not static. This is a woman caught up in the flow of life. She is in touch with both the inner and outer worlds and gains truth from both. Her intent is for wholeness, and each day, with quiet determination, she keeps to her plan.

LIBRA
(September 24–October 23)

Your Essential Self

RULED BY VENUS, THE PLANET OF BEAUTY, GRACE AND creativity, Libra women are blessed by the gods. A sensitivity to beauty and harmony, along with a strong intelligence and sense of humor makes them desirable friends and companions. Highly imaginative and having great taste, Libra women can create beautiful environments in which everything harmonizes and complements everything else.

Libra women want their world to be beautiful and feel compelled to conjure beauty utilizing their extraordinary sense of color and style. Likewise, they have a poise and natural sense of what is appropriate in every situation. Because of this, they make spectacular hostesses, entertaining with style, elegance and graciousness.

Perhaps, like no other sign, Libra women know the art of pleasing. They also want to be liked and loved. Therefore, they are careful to show their very best face to the world. Armed with that, impeccable manners, and a strong sense of propriety and decorum, they easily impress upon the world the fact that they are very attractive people.

Libra women are also extremely smart, talented, fast learners who have the potential of achieving a great deal in a lifetime. Libra is also the sign of law and Libran women not only make great lawyers, but great negotiators in any situation. The only thing that holds them back is insecurity based on a lack of self-confidence—something no one, on first meeting, would ever believe was possible.

Nevertheless, this is an invisible cart that they do tend to carry around behind. Libra women are highly impressionable and ready to be impressed with others. Yet, when it comes to assigning that same power to themselves, they writhe around in confusion, often having problems making the right decisions for themselves, second-guessing themselves and doing a great deal of "to-ing" and "fro-ing." Libra women usually act extremely humble. However, this apparent humility is really a mask for something more profound—a deep distrust of their own power. This usually causes a great deal of pain in life as I discuss in detail in a later section under the dark side of the personality. However, suffice it to say now, that despite all of her enormous talents, the Libra woman does not have a happy home in her own soul and is forever seeking support from the outside.

An idealist to the core, and quite a perfectionist, she wants everything to be glossy. Indeed, she wants life to be the prettiest of pictures and suffers terribly if caught in the close company of the sort of crude, ugly people that do unfortunately, populate a portion of the world. Her idealism is brought to everything that is important to her, whether it be her work, her projects, her relationships, or her place in the overall scheme of things. The Libra woman wants it all and wants every piece to fit together in perfect proportions. She is an architect of ideas, a visionary of sorts, however, the problem is that sometimes in this less than ideal world, her ideas cannot be accomplished according to her timing and rarefied set of standards and conditions.

She sees things as they ought to be, not necessarily as they can be. Creatively, this can be very frustrating. It can also mean that there is often a struggle involved in achieving a desired outcome that takes away from the beauty of the process. Libra women can't bear bumps and don't easily put them behind themselves. They want everything to be smooth and simply wonderful which is a source of the unhappiness seen so often in this sign.

As with any person who has a strong Venusian influence in the chart, Libras can be very self-indulgent. When frustrated, their needs, fears and insecurities can take over. And these needs and gut-wrenching insecurities are the shadow of that wonderful, smiling face, so eager to please and so pleasing.

These are the two basic sides of the Libra woman: the need to give because of an instinctual understanding of the sharing process and a self-absorbed, self-centeredness that blows everything out of proportion. Needless to say, this is complex and it is this complexity that can be the source of conflicts that come to form the core of her personality. The Libra woman has to grow into herself. She has to learn how to trust herself and develop confidence in the areas of her life that keep giving her trouble. However, she also has to be more realistic about some of the limitations that come up against her. Life is not and never will be the ideal place she wants it to be. However, it is up to her to make it meaningful.

The Libra woman naturally embodies so many gifts of the Goddess: love, beauty, sensitivity, intuition, imagination, creativity. However, before she can fully benefit from her gifts, she has to learn how to give to herself. She must not allow her gifts to stagnate waiting for another to help her. Her light must light her own unique way. And even in times of darkness, she must learn how to trust that light and treat it with respect, care and confidence.

Your Dark Side

THE SUN SYMBOLIZES OUR SELF, OUR EGO AND OUR SENSE of identity. The sun is in its fall in Libra, which means that there is a weak sense of self. The self doesn't fully trust itself. It doesn't feel complete by itself. This issue is at the root of the Libran experience of life and it can be a painful one.

Libra is also the zodiac sign associated with the natural seventh house which has to do with relationships, partnerships and significant others. The focus of the consciousness is others, often to the exclusion of oneself. Therefore, the impending life question that keeps coming up again and again is "What is my worth *alone,* without a relationship?"

Libran woman often seem perched on an edge, waiting for an insight, inspiration or bastion of support to spur them on. In the meantime, because they don't trust their own inner voice or themselves, they can easily be thrown off course by other people or their own negative emotions. And when the atmosphere of this cloud passes away, what is left can be a lot of confusion. So often the Libran woman holds on to this confusion as if that's all that she has. And when she holds on too long, it starts to feel so familiar and alive that gradually she begins to mistake it for her identity.

Libra is both a highly intelligent and creative sign that has enormous potential. The problem comes with how to make the best use of this potential. There is also another problem: Often Libran women don't want to use it as much as they want to be lulled, nurtured and supported by someone else. They want a shoulder, womb, mommy, daddy, powerful husband who will keep the ugly, nasty world at bay. And they often put more energy into trying to find this than they do trying to realize themselves. The difficulties of this syndrome are compounded by cultural conditioning. To be an independent woman in this society is still, by no means, an easy task. And despite a great deal of social change that has taken place over the past twenty years, it is still a patriarchal society fueled by competitive male values which tend to try to control women rather than encourage them. Many Libran women find it easy on one level to fall in step with the limitations of the system that also undermines them. What they don't see at the outset is the price that has to be paid down the road—and there always is a price. At the very least, the price is a sacrifice of their positive, powerful selfhood. This encompasses not only the expression of who they distinctly are, but also who they must one day be—for themselves.

Because this flip-flop involvement between themselves and others pervades so many issues in their lives so deeply, it also robs Libras of a strong, necessary sense of self-esteem. And the insidious, circular problem is that the more they feel this absence of a core self-esteem, the more they are prone to be dependent on others.

This problem is compounded by a basic lack of certainty and sense of conviction which comes from seeing two sides of a situation simultaneously. This ability is actually a strength and at its best, can lead to powerful, insightful thinking that takes all factors into consideration. Further, it can also aid the sort of understanding that can lead to its own wisdom, the wisdom that comes from being able to get to truth through a process of deliberation.

However, first of all, Libran women have to stop thinking of themselves as incomplete, as vessels in search of some filler or as dependent on someone outside of themselves; that is, they have to stop thinking of themselves as having a self that has to be dealt with. I cannot tally the number of times I have watched highly intelligent and talented Libran women writhe in a self-created darkness that denied the existence of their enormous gifts, giving themselves over to an internal voice that completely undermined them. However, it is important to remember, that as women, we all have the self-doubting, self-deprecating voices we have to deal with, the voices that are only too eager to tell us that we are too fat or will fail or come too far short of the mark to make any real difference. The trick is to challenge that voice, to dialogue with it, talk back to it, ask it questions, develop a relationship with it instead of becoming it.

To get on top of that negative fear voice which is the voice of the unconscious, takes disciplined practice. And it is part of the Venusian nature to want things to not only be beautiful but easy. Librans with very strong Saturns in their charts are inspiring in their ability to stick to things until they see the positive results. However, when the pleasure principle overrides the discipline, there is a tendency to want positive change to occur as if by the good fate of magic. The result is a spiritual laziness. It is common to sit down with a Libran woman in this state and address the issue of what is impeding her, offering insightful suggestions of solutions—only to have each one met with complete resistance. This is the truly frustrating aspect of this sign—not only does this type of Libran woman want to stay stuck, but she wants to pull others into her stuck place so she won't have to sit there alone.

Often in life, things have to get worse before they get better. And the Libran woman must go through her malaise completely and alone if she is going to be transformed by it. What she stands to learn from the experience is her own power—that something wonderful is there, an intelligence, an energy, a purely creative spirit that is all hers alone. It is waiting for her to claim it, own it, use it and share it with the world. The world is lit up by Libran gifts. If Libran women could only see how much, they would suffer much less.

However, sometimes it takes a crisis to crack the pattern of self-abnegation. It always seem to require a certain degree of suffering, although it does not *have to*. What is often required is a sacrifice of the past, the fear and pain of the past. The hard part, of course, is that the future is still unknown. It is unfolding.

In this place between past and future, which often becomes an abyss which seems insurmountable, the darkness can be overwhelming. Air signs expect things to unfold in a linear fashion. However, in the life of the soul, time unfolds like a spiral. There is a going upward and a going downward and perhaps a staying in a certain place for a while to emotionally assimilate. What this means in a Libra woman's life is that often her will and intellect will say one thing and her life another. This can be very painful and confusing. She is reasonable and she wants to live through her reason. However, the path of her soul can thwart this. It can pull her in a completely different direction, one that she is not prepared for and that may frighten her. At such a time, she must surrender. This is a time of her unfolding to the next level. She must allow this and trust that there is a meaning to the darkness. It will bring her something beautiful if she will just be patient and take responsibility for herself—which means stop expecting others to help her live her life. The Libra woman must take responsibility for her own life. The more she clings to the bastions of support she has created on the outside, the longer it will take. At a certain point she has to begin to nurture herself.

This reminds me of a Libra friend whose up-and-down relationship finally ended. She called me and told me that she was suicidal. I knew, of course, that she wasn't suicidal. I knew that she was just a Libra. I did her the biggest favor. I did not coddle her or treat her like the poor baby she wanted to be. I just let her talk and talk herself into a state of complete emotional exhaustion. Then her emotional energy shifted. She reemerged from this quite chipper and childlike, talking about how wonderful it was to have all the space in her closets back which inspired her to go shopping. Her suicidal dialogues were like a thought she had in the third grade. She had finally given up all that stuff and was facing herself and many things she wanted to do with herself. Crisis had forced this to happen. In the process, she changed so much for the better. Later on she admitted that she knew the relationship had to die but for a long time her mind kept struggling against it.

Libra women have a wonderful sense of humor and irony. The healthy detachment in humor is the same detachment needed to help them through their negativity. The negativity is only a voice, a voice most creative people have. But those thoughts are energy, energy that has to be transformed. Libra women have to work on directing their thoughts instead of allowing their thoughts to direct them. It all begins here—with their relationships with their own minds. Their selves, light or dark, are the continual outgrowth of their thoughts. Their thoughts are their consciousness and it can be a consciousness that is like a magnet for all they want their life to become.

Your Approach to Love

LIBRA WOMEN ARE IN LOVE WITH LOVE AND ALL ITS ROmantic trappings. Falling in love is their idea of something very exciting to do. And however it ends up, that's how it starts out—as an idea.

Libra women think a great deal about love. But that

doesn't mean that they're deeply emotional. It merely means that they think a great deal about love.

Libra is an air sign and air has to do with thinking and fantasizing. Libra women think that it would be so nice to share someone's life, it would be so nice to have someone supportive be there for them, it would be so nice to have a relationship so they wouldn't have to be alone. Love, like a law school degree, seems to make a lot of things possible. However, because this is an air sign, there can also be a curious detachment. Partners can often be seen more in terms of their role than their personhood and own set of needs and problems. For instance, I knew one Libra woman who confessed she married her husband because he was a great dance partner. This is a pretty extreme example and needless to say, the relationship didn't last. However, this is not the only time I have witnessed how superficial the emotions can run in this sign.

Often Libra women just don't know what they want, so they think that a relationship will solve that. Like Taurus, this is a sign that tends to overvalue love and romance and to look at its potential pleasures in advertising terms. However, there is also something else at work here. This is also the sign associated with the natural seventh house of the horoscope which is the house of marriage and partnership. Therefore, Libra women often feel that to find themselves, they must first give themselves away.

Libra women tend to get desperate without a relationship. The exceptions to this are the Librans who have gone this route too many times only to learn something crucial about themselves—and that is that they still have to deal with themselves and when they don't deal with themselves, they stand to suffer immeasurably through a relationship.

The seventh house is really about equal sharing, not about escaping oneself through another. And this is the lesson in love that so many Libra women need to learn. It is always possible to find this kind of escape if one is that desperate. However, the personal price is very high. Furthermore, when you escape yourself in another, the person receiving you will never treat you as a gift. It is only a matter of time until you are taken for granted.

The Libran woman has to first develop a relationship with herself before she can have a successful relationship with a life partner. That is her great challenge: to take responsibility for herself and not protect herself. The Libra woman who is able to bring a complete self to a relationship instead of trying to escape herself is the one who is able to use her femininity to generate a connection that is creative, vital and lasting. The relationship she has first with herself will become, in a sense, her fate. From that mirror all will be reflected.

Your Power Source

LIBRA WOMEN ARE BORN WITH A SENSE OF BEAUTY that is the source of a great creative imagination. Beauty brings us possibility. It forces us to open our eyes wider to see more and take in more. Libra women can enhance life through their ability to conjure beauty in great detail. Through their highly refined esthetic, they can transform an environment into a breathtaking experience that is completely embracing.

Libra women are also extremely thoughtful and gracious. As hostesses they have a way of making everything perfect, from the dinner itself to the details of its presentation. Their natural poise and sociability make them excel at making others feel comfortable and entertained. Libra women can be so charming, witty and wonderful that dinner guests won't want to go home.

Libra women are also the first ones with follow-up. Appreciative phone calls the day after a dinner and beautiful, gracious notes for all occasions are typical of their old-world feminine style. With special touches they make others feel special. In little ways they can bring sunbeams into someone else's boring day.

Appreciative of all the beauty and the best in life, Libra women know how to make magic. Creative in everything they seriously undertake, they enliven life with their vision. The Libra woman can actually make living an art. It starts with all her small careful choices and ends in an atmosphere, garden, work of art that transports the mind far and away from the colorless and trivial.

Her precise sense of elegance lends an aura of grandeur to both her person and her home. And within her home her decorating and entertaining style says so much about what life might be with the right taste and meticulous attention to detail. With everything she does, she brings her acute sensibility that says "yes!" to all the beauty in life.

Through her heightened perceptions she can transform the mundane into the magical. In dark, insecure moments she must always remember the power that lies in her own creative mind—and she must use it to enlarge her own life.

Supersmart, articulate and a gifted diplomat, she often uses her gifts to please others. However, her enormous and highly versatile creativity should also bring light into her own life. The Libra woman can be a luminous reminder to the world around her of the sacred beauty of the everyday, of the way that we must look at the world to really see the Goddess and her many offerings, the artistry within our own souls that lies waiting to be touched and felt and written and heard.

SCORPIO

(October 24–November 22)

Your Essential Self

EMOTIONAL DEPTH IS WHAT DEFINES THE SCORPIO woman and everything in her experience of life springs from that. The most complex sign of the zodiac, she is a confluence of emotion, will, perception, intuition, moodiness and deep inner yearning. The Scorpio woman is so many things at once that she has earned the reputation of mysterious. Mystery, however, is not something she consciously tries to create, although she is conscious about keeping an emotional distance from many people and revealing herself selectively or not at all. Scorpio does this because she is very private and has to feel her way into situations and people. Since her most profound desire is to connect on an emotionally deep level that has personal meaning, she has few really close friends with whom she shares her soul.

Scorpio women "know" things. They perceive, they intuit, they empathize, they understand. They also have remarkable memories that put every detail in place and keep them filed away in their minds for future reference. A certain soulful loneliness comes from the awareness that there are so few other people that they can share life with on all of their levels.

Because this is such an inwardly focused sign and one so often isolated from others, Scorpio women are more accustomed to talking to themselves inside their heads than they are talking deeply to anybody else. Their emotional moods, fears and complications are so layered and entangled that they are not readily communicated, especially to someone who is talking and thinking on a much more superficial level. So she nods, gives polite responses, her eyes glaze over and no one is aware that she is only partially present. If she cannot be with a deep, soul-related connection, she would often rather be alone in her own inner world.

However, that inner world brings its own loneliness. In the throes of such loneliness her mind can turn in on her and make her moody, fearful and compulsive. Because this is a sign of such emotional intensity, the Scorpio woman needs to get her feelings out and let a lot of the negativity go. She needs to be able to hear herself speak. This has a very different effect than hearing her own inner mental thoughts. The spoken words speak back to her as if she were hearing them for the first time. The result can bring a lot of self-awareness and insight.

As the sign of death and rebirth, the Scorpio woman goes through many life cycles, separations and endings on many levels. The pain she feels from the separations leaves her with a deep-seated fear of abandonment. It also makes her wise, aware and insightful.

Through the journey of her life, the Scorpio woman comes to understand the meaning of the word *process*—going through something slowly, too slowly for the comfort of the ego, but coming out the other end at least a wiser, deeper, different person.

During their difficult times, Scorpio women need to go down within themselves in a very reflective and contemplative way. By doing this, their darkness can be transformed from pain to awareness and meaning. Sometimes this meaning takes a long time to surface. However, this is not always the case. What is important to remember is when that meaning is deeply desired, it does come and it can bring wisdom, power and emotional/psychic energy that can be life enhancing.

It is essential for the Scorpio woman to allow her fear to bring her to a deeper level within herself. She can do this by slowing down when she is upset, by taking a bath, getting into bed and staring at the moon or reading poetry, listening to music (something like Chopin's Nocturnes) and sipping some tea, taking a long walk in the woods, reflecting by the water, acting out through art and painting her mood. Playing uplifting music, lighting candles and not thinking but letting the intuition take over and then writing in a journal is great food for the soul as well. But Scorpio also has to go through the pain of her darkness to get beyond it. That often involves crying her eyes out or trusting the process of her depression—knowing that something within her is dying off and a new level of consciousness is struggling to be born.

It is the nature of this sign that the dying/rebirth process will happen many times and on many different levels in a lifetime. This is also the key to Scorpio power. The Scorpio woman can be a wise crone at an early age because her all-or-nothing nature will often bring her into experiences where her conscious personality is dramatically and powerfully transformed.

With her obsessive, compulsive mentality Scorpio also evokes her own inner demons and, in the process, has to straddle the inner and the outer world. The demons may be rage, resentment, fear, anxiety, festered hurt or a deadened feeling that simply swoops over her in a mood. When these demons appear, they claim a great deal of psychic energy and make it difficult for Scorpio to keep up the cool, cheery facade that the outer world seems to demand. Letting go is an extraordinary challenge for Scorpio. This is because there is a distrust of what might be left if one lets go. Rightly so, Scorpio is capable of deep psychological pain, just as her potential is profound psychological/ spiritual brilliance. To claim this luminous power, however, there is no route for Scorpio other than the heroic journey through her own underworld. Often, with this sign, there is no choice but to let things fall mysteriously into place and allow destiny to take over.

Love, sex and relationships play a central part in Scorpio's picture. The sexuality of a Scorpio woman is a very deep thing but does not merely involve momentary physical gratification. A Scorpio woman's sexuality reflects her need for intimate connection and passion. Because her need for passion is so great, intense affairs have the potential of becoming addictive. If, on the other hand, an encounter has no sexual chemistry but is merely affable, the Scorpio woman is bored and cut off. The psychological power of the erotic enlivens her—even if this power or person is dangerous. The erotic force can overtake her rational mind completely and possess her. The power of such a connection can seem mythic and for a while well worth the sacrifice of sanity. But only for a while. A force deep within the Scorpio nature forces things to conclusions and relationships either start to live on a deeper level or they die—often with as much negative feeling as there was passion.

Although on the outside the Scorpio woman maintains a cool, in-control persona, deep inside she often desires to lose herself to something more vast. The erotic relationship is one area. For the artist, there is also the relationship with her art, and for the mystically inclined Scorpio woman, there is the relationship with the divine. Although the Scorpio woman can achieve divine ecstasy through sex, ultimately she has to stop projecting her own desire for the divine onto a relationship or man and experience it from within if she is going to attain her authentic spiritual power.

The life of a Scorpio woman is a journey that often takes her through many transitions. Everything along the way is meaningful and can lead her to the Source. There is often pain involved in Scorpio's experiences but the pain has to do with not seeing what she has to see for herself to move on to a higher level. There is also excitement. The excitement Scorpio finds dwells in the mystery of herself which is always being revealed to her as long as she is determined to discover it. All Scorpio has to do is trust in her own process, respect its sacredness and pray to the Goddess within to help her get on with it—always going deeper, always transforming and transcending her old self.

Your Dark Side

As deep as a Scorpio woman is, she can be equally dark. Her episodic darkness—the moodiness and depressions that creep up and get her from behind—seem to be the price she has to pay for having such depth in a society with such shallow values.

The Scorpio woman is intuitive, psychic and emotionally receptive. She absorbs other people's pain like a sponge and she holds on to her own feelings for a very long time. When something happens that disturbs her, she goes down into it, obsessively runs it through her mind and looks at it from every perspective. This *can* lead to a deeper understanding but it can also go to nowhere but a pool of negative thoughts that can engulf her. In the extreme it can lead to depression and emotional paralysis.

Scorpio must always beware of being engulfed by her own intense emotions. It is why order and control are so important to her in the outer world. They are a defense against impending chaos from within. At the same time, power is a significant issue in this sign. Scorpio women have tremendous willpower, a disgust with weakness and a steely determination to rise above anything. This can cause them to deny their wounds, burying them under an inhuman work schedule, exercise routine, or high-power success goals.

The problem is that these Band-Aids only work for a time. The unconscious has its own power, regardless of what the ego demands, and the murky stuff of the unconscious will surface, often when it's least expected. Therefore, it is common for the Scorpio woman not even to know that she is angry until she gets depressed. This is because the anger is so deeply buried. When this anger does show itself, it is like the Hydra, the many headed serpent in mythology—every time you cut off one head, another grows back in its place. How does one get to the source of the pain and not be engulfed by it?

There is not an easy answer. As a matter of fact, few emotional answers come easily in this complex sign. It all takes time and often a gifted psychotherapist. Scorpio women themselves make gifted psychotherapists; their personal understanding of human complexity, along with their powerful intuition, enables them to get to the source of people's emotional pain.

The Scorpio woman's insight, compassion and capacity for love are great strengths in her character. However, when the need for power gets in the way of the ability to love, the Scorpio woman has a serious problem. She has cut herself off from her own feminine Source.

The fate of the Scorpio woman is determined by the fact that she is fixed water—which means fixed emotions. Once an emotion or an opinion has taken hold, she cannot change course easily because she sees her course as truth. Therefore, when she acts out of manipulation and is determined to have power over someone else, she can become dangerously entwined in her own manipulations, which usually come back on her in negative ways.

The dark side of Scorpio can be very self-destructive and psychologically addictive. Scorpio is the sign of death and transformation and it often seems that to obtain their authentic power, Scorpios must go through an essential death and transformation experience. This painful process often seems to be the only way Scorpios can reach the kind of transcendent wisdom of which they are capable.

Scorpio is a sign of extremes and inner compulsions. The tides of inner emotional intensity can be consuming when turned in the direction of addictions, sexual involvements or vengeances. Forgiveness is not a strength in this sign. When wronged, Scorpios want justice. This combined with Scorpio's trademark intensity can get those born under this sign into some trouble. Scorpio women need to be aware of this and not let their compulsions get the better of them.

The most important thing for Scorpios to keep in mind during difficult challenges and transitions is that there is meaning to be gained through their struggles. That meaning will lead Scorpios to great inner power if they allow it to reveal itself to them. A Scorpio can do that by trusting that everything is a process and every process has a purpose. The purpose is to bring her closer to her divine self, the self that is able to see the whole picture—the higher as well as the lower, the light as well as the darkness. There is no quick fix, no easy route. Scorpios have to go through themselves, go through their processes and *trust* them, trust that they are taking them somewhere they need to be. Scorpios must see their life as a journey. At different stages of the journey the Scorpio woman will be a different person and want different things and people. She shouldn't be so fixed about thinking who she might be or what she might want. Enjoy the awakening bit by bit. But always be clear that all your experiences are taking you to what you have to know. Allow the clearing away of emotional debris so that the inner light gets brighter and leads to greater joy and love and meaning. The Scorpio legacy is power, not power *over* but power from *within*. Scorpio darkness leads to that power. Deep within that darkness is the authentic truth. Go to its Source.

Your Approach to Love

SCORPIO WOMEN COME ALIVE THROUGH FATAL SEXUAL attractions. If asked what originally sparked the attraction, she might say it was his penetrating eyes, his voice or the way he moved his body. But actually she's just guessing. While it probably is true that she was magnetized to some of his physical characteristics, it's more likely that her unconscious also played a big part. While Scorpio is identified as the sign of sex, it is not sex alone that the Scorpio woman is interested in—it is an emotional intensity that is so deeply aroused in her that it must express itself physically. Passion captivates the Scorpio woman, not emotionally divorced sex. When she is deeply involved, sex becomes a profound, mysterious experience that can overtake her life.

There is a desire deep within the Scorpio woman to be so intensely and totally aroused that she is possessed. When a Scorpio woman is overtaken by passion, she feels totally alive, even if that passion involves pain. And once she has experienced that— even if it is with the wrong person, it is terribly difficult to shut off.

That is why the love experience can be so dangerous for this sign and why, in its darkest moments, love can become addiction. Scorpio is the sign of extremes known for its all-or-nothing intensity. The problem with this kind of intense passion is that, first of all, it has a dark side of hatred, and second, it can completely overtake the conscious mind and bring about some very irrational behavior.

Scorpio is a sign of inherent strength and discipline. However, when the deep, intense emotions are evoked in the wrong way, a kind of momentary madness can overtake the personality. It is common for deeply wounded Scorpio women to withdraw into their wound for a time with no energy left for life. However, after they get their strength back, watch out! This is a woman who never forgets the depth of her pain and who is very capable of revenge, which she will be tempted to pursue in her own unique way. Sometimes the revenge is wrought on life and she never allows herself to feel quite so deeply. This is not necessarily a conscious decision. The Scorpio woman may just find after being deeply hurt that she's just not strongly attracted to anyone for a long period of time.

Sexual involvement can be many things to this deep, complicated woman. It can mean power "over" or it can mean losing power to someone appearing more powerful. It can be erotic and passionate or very emotionally painful. However, one thing it always is is psychological.

Scorpio women can become enslaved by their own unconscious impulses as well as by the unconscious impulses of the man with whom they are involved. This is Scorpio's ultimate danger point—losing themselves. They must always maintain a reasonable amount of control as a psychological safety net. Being obsessive and compulsive by nature, Scorpio has to be aware of her thoughts and emotions and not allow their focus to consume all rational thought. Likewise,

Scorpio women should never allow fear and neediness to make them compromise their own life.

Scorpios can easily lose their balance and control in the intense relationships they tend to attract. When that balance is lost and the emotions brim over the edge, a destructive situation is the result. Sometimes, perhaps often in life, that can't be helped. However, what is most important is that the Scorpio woman put the pain and the joy in perspective and see herself as an active participant in the relationship that she wanted. Even if it turned out to be a very painful experience, she should view it as a rite of passage in which things had to be learned to bring her to a new place within herself. The powerful Scorpio woman is the one who wants to be powerful in her full womanhood. She will take the time to go within herself to work on gaining a deeper understanding of herself and her process. Hopefully, this will bring her to a depth of awareness that will prevent her from repeating old mistakes and establishing a pattern that has a stranglehold on her life and her energies. The deeper and larger view of herself is what is most important, whether she is happily married or miserably in love. Unfortunately, it is often misery that brings us to our awakenings and goads us on to a deeper awareness of ourselves. The Scorpio woman's power is that of the old wise crone who has passed through all experience—the light and the dark. She has lived it all, understands it all and is in a strange way, still with it but beyond it. She is beyond herself, a self she has earned, living through a wisdom she has gained that is powerful and ever wondrous.

Your Power Source

SCORPIO IS FOCUSED ON POWER, SOUL POWER. WITHIN that power realm, both darkness and light come into play. In Scorpio the relationship between light and darkness is deeply interwoven like an intricate tapestry. In order to get to the light of the spirit, one has to go through the tunnel of darkness, the darkness of the unconscious. The more one lives unconsciously, the darker and denser the world appears. Petty perspectives are all-powerful and the sense of "I" is submerged in society at large which snuffs out one's sense of individuality and authenticity.

From the moment she is born, the Scorpio woman is on a journey through her consciousness. Her deep, complex nature demands her conscious attention. She gets pulled within through her moods and intense emotional feelings. The journey begins when she tries to understand what her moods mean, when she wants to know more about that inner self that is mysterious even to her. Some Scorpio women are old souls at a very early age. Even without a great deal of worldly experience, they speak with a wisdom and depth of understanding.

As life progresses, challenges will spring up and provide tests for the Scorpio woman. Each test has its own meaning. Each test is a portal to soul power, wisdom and profound insight. Each test will provide an ending of sorts and an ensuing sense of renewal which is usually accompanied by a heightened feeling of being alive. If there is a specific mythological goddess associated with this sign, it is Persephone, the goddess who was kidnapped by Pluto, god of the underworld. Her fate was to live in Hades for six months, emerging to bring new life to the earth, creating spring. Archetypally, the Scorpio woman goes through similar cycles during her lifetime. There are the cycles of mood changes and cycles of life changes. Overall, the pattern of the Scorpio life is a spiral. There are ups and downs, periods of stagnation and periods of illumination. The years before forty are the hardest because there are a lot of psychological and emotional growing pains. Pluto rules this sign and Pluto is the slowest moving and the most mysterious planet in the zodiac. Pluto is involved with emotional processes and deep spiritual/psychological transformation. Pluto also symbolizes mystery, the mystery of life and death, and the mystery of the soul speaking through the persona.

The Scorpio woman's power unfolds when she begins to realize that events have a higher meaning in her life. Pain usually brings her to a place where she is forced to sit down and sort out the debris from a deep disappointment or loss. Her first response to this sort of pain is usually a mentally obsessive downward swing in which her mind moves in circles and her whole inner being feels trapped in darkness. Scorpio is the most intense sign and, therefore, emotional pain can be a deathlike experience that can swamp the ego. However, this darkness is also a potential time for inner knowing, a time when the Goddess quietly speaks. The Scorpio woman must always look for the meaning of her experiences. When she is able to look at an experience for what it is telling her about herself—and all experiences are saying something—then she will be able to get messages that reveal what she needs to know to make important changes.

Picasso was a Scorpio and his paintings reflect his complex and profound view of the world. The painting

Guernica is not pretty. It is dark and frightening. Nevertheless, it is rich and deep and wise. It is also truth. Such is the consciousness of the Scorpio woman. That range, that depth, that ability to perceive truth is power. A Scorpio woman has to grow into her power. But first, she must own it. The worst thing she can do to herself is try to escape it, walk away from it or give it away. And the number one way many Scorpio women try to do this is through men.

Scorpio women get destructively caught up in men in two ways. They seek self-validation through their relationships with them and they attempt to get power from trying to play out the role of a man's sexual fantasy. I deal with the love issue in another section but suffice it to say here that in both of these roles the Scorpio woman loses a self she cannot afford to lose. Her power from within is her sole source of strength. This is what will sustain her if and when everything else disappears.

When a Scorpio woman has the courage and integrity to be herself and grow into more of herself without role-playing or manipulations, she is ready to realize her real power, power from "within." At a certain point, she has to come home to this place herself and discover what is there as well as what one day might be. She does herself a grave injustice if she stagnates in a lifeless relationship or lives through the mode of manipulator. Her life should be a constant unfolding, layer by layer, that allows her to express more and more of her creativity and spirituality. She must learn to let her depths speak and to respond to them wisely. She must also open herself to the answers and messages that are all around her, the metaphors in everyday experience that will begin to have a synchronistic effect on her life. When she does all this, her intuition will heighten, her life will gain in meaning and there will be a place within herself that will become a very wise, ancient Source of truth and understanding. That is power. It is her potential. And it is boundless.

SAGITTARIUS
(November 23–December 21)

Your Essential Self

LIKE AN ARROW MOVING THROUGH SPACE, THE FEMALE Archer is always traveling in a significant direction, whether the journey be physical, intellectual or philosophical. The energy of motion is always with the Sagittarian woman even if it is from a purely cerebral activity.

Fueled by her ideals, an insatiable curiosity and an intense love of learning, the female Sagittarius delights in diverse pursuits and in the beneficent aspect of change. There are times when she may appear flighty. She probably is. Brimming with energy and ideas, she doesn't know when to stop or how. What's new and exciting and unexplained calls her name—and sometimes that gets in the way of everything else.

Boring, mundane duties and tasks are not the Sagittarian's forte. Neither is patience or putting up graciously with boorish people. The Sagittarian woman is the spontaneous sort who often speaks before considering the possible impact of her words. This is one woman who needs to mentally edit.

Caught up in the moment, the Sagittarian woman doesn't notice whatever else may be around her. She operates so far ahead of herself that the present quickly fades into the past. She is highly future oriented and becomes bright-eyed when she's looking forward to something. Her sense of infinite possibility is almost religious. Anything that seriously dampens her optimistic outlook diminishes the light of her spirit. However, it must be said that she simply does not allow anything to bring her down for long.

The Sagittarian woman was born to break chains that bind—or so she thinks. Constraints and constrictions are not her style and she won't politely endure them. The freedom to be and to become all that she can possibly think up is her personal raison d'être. To not try everything that appeals to her at least once is to live a life that is painfully dull. The Sagittarian woman is alive with the excitement of life itself. Optimistic and expansive, she also has a big supply of foolhardy courage. This can save her in the dark times but it can also do her in. The Sagittarian woman cannot really comprehend how to be cautious and careful. All that security-oriented stuff is for some other sign. She's happier in the jungle petting poisonous snakes and, of course, living to tell everyone about it.

The woman born under this sign may exaggerate her stories a bit for the full effect. She is a scintillating storyteller, especially when the subject of her stories is some insane mishap. Her uproarious sense of humor adds so much sparkle to her stories that no one really minds if some of the details are more than slightly off-kilter. She doesn't tell slanted stories purposely, it's just that her memory gets a little hazy at times, especially at those times when a little exaggeration would enlarge a story.

The Sagittarian woman's sense of time is rather strange and quite subjective. Everything to her is so relative that everything is sort of true depending on how she chooses to look at it and what day it happens to be and what the weather might be like. One should never argue with a Sagittarian. Not only will you never win, but along the way you can become so hopelessly confused that you come away like Alice in Wonderland. The most amazing and amusing thing about the Sagittarian woman's perspective is that in midstream she often changes her mind. Therefore, to hold her tightly to any one of her statements is like trying to grab water. She can't be locked into anything and you have to take her just as you find her.

On the other hand, she is both enormously intelligent and insightful. The problem is she's not always *right*—although she's convinced she is. The Sagittarian woman takes great pride in both her knowledge and her opinions. And this terribly righteous quality can, at times, become a bit overbearing. The good part is that the Sagittarian mind is a fluid mind that doesn't get stuck in one groove so long that it becomes boring. Likewise, her sense of humor usually lightens up the weight of her opinions so the conversation flows.

Whether you like them or agree with them or think them simply "know-it-alls," Sagittarian women have flair. Flair for being adventurous and amusing, daring and dauntless. They also have a flair for finding what's interesting in a small town or an overcrowded city. Their minds are always tuning into something with a sense of discovery. And they are always on the verge of some momentous realization or meaningful encounter. The only way a Sagittarian woman can become bored is to be confined and forced into a situation where she can't freely express herself.

This confinement often occurs in relationships. The Sagittarian woman—mouth, mind and all—is not the dream ideal of some insecure man who can't bear to be challenged. She is also not for someone who would live in a state of daily dread at the thought of what she might do next. Naturally, anyone who would attempt to leash her would find the task similar to dragging a leopard to a tea party.

Sagittarian women have to sow a few very wild oats and roam through some men before settling down with anyone. They are like the goddess Diana, who was really in love with her own spirit. At its best, the marvelous, life-affirming Sagittarian spirit is highly spiritual. Its essence is faith, a humble respect for the mystery of life and the desire to somehow participate in that mystery in a way that is transforming and transcendent. She is also interested in sharing that meaning with others so that all are enlarged by the light.

The Sagittarian woman who is typical of her sign is on a quest for truth. She must be growing and developing to derive a sustaining sense of self-satisfaction. She is also one to become impassioned by such causes as ecology, the underprivileged or animal rights. She can be a strident doer who follows her ideals or a thinker who is forever stretching her intellect. Whatever her involvement, it is always from the heart— even, if in a lifetime, she should have many changes of heart. This is part of her expansive nature that requires change, diversity and sometimes digression. The Sagittarian woman is capable of changing course just as she can change opinions. A captivating interest, circumstance or situation is always popping up at just the right time for her. The combination of her curiosity and need for stimulation sends her scurrying to more than one source.

That is one element of Sagittarian magic. Another is a sense of humor that could charm serpents. Sagittarian women see what's funny and have a talent for transforming the ponderous and overly serious into something terribly silly. Instinctively they understand when some emotional distance can be an essential thing. After all, this is the sign of the higher mind. And even with an unsteady aim, in the course of a lifetime, they're always shooting higher and higher.

Your Dark Side

SAGITTARIANS ARE SELDOM DARK. HOWEVER, THEY are capable of being very foolish on occasion. And this kind of behavior can bring on its own dark ramifications.

The Sagittarian woman is Jupiter's child and Jupiter can be a planet of excess, play and irresponsibility. It usually takes Sagittarius a good while to grow up. An immature Jupiterian doesn't take things seriously, most of all, rules. However, she finds it fun to see how far she can go to break them and get away with it.

In the early years, the Sagittarius shows the requisite flighty, flaky behavior like cutting school, experimenting with drugs and leaving any number of people stranded and simply furious. Jupiter, her ruler, is linked with beliefs which include a fairly long list of false ones. A typical immature Jupiterian belief is the necessity of freedom at all costs and the moral imperative to break imposed boundaries. Under this umbrella lies a big conviction: "The word *no* does not apply to me."

In the early years Sagittarians go out to play in the world with all that in mind and have to get hit on the head by life. (These are the fortunate ones.) The ones who get away with just enough things to never learn, also never change or grow. As adults they are scattered, unfocused and their energy is diffused. They have a history of a plethora of unfinished projects, each begun with a characteristic flourish and a lot of talk, only to be ultimately abandoned and forgotten like a lunchtime friend from third grade.

The negative side of Sagittarius is a feckless one with no staying power. They do only what they like and drop it the moment their enthusiasm wanes. Life is too short to stick to anything too boring is the belief here. Why should a Sagittarian follow through with the miserable dirty work that follows the initial idea, they wonder.

Procrastination is a dark Sagittarian game; so is complete avoidance. The demonic thing about avoidance is that all those horrible, nasty, nitty-gritty things that must be avoided never go away. Instead, these things have an insidious way of getting in the way of Sagittarian accomplishment. Unless there are Capricorn or earth planets to be found elsewhere in the chart, the values of responsibility and discipline are slowly learned for those born under this sign.

The pleasure principle is a strong one for Sagittarius. This is probably why Sagittarians are so much fun. It is in their nature to enjoy and to take that enjoyment to the limits. Naturally, too much of this self-indulgence leads to complete sloth. And in sloth there is no light. As a matter of fact, in deep sloth there is deep darkness and pain.

Our lessons have to be learned for the light of spirit to shine through. And Sagittarius is a sign focused on light—having it and spreading it. I once knew a brilliant multitalented Sagittarius who was the funniest person I had ever met. This person was also the most chronically depressed person I had known. She was trapped within this huge personality, focused on mulling over the most emotionally immature beliefs and in the process, accumulating more and more debt. She was also given to passionately pursuing interests that she would later drift away from, having nothing in the end to show for herself. That such a gifted person, a potential bearer of light, could be so black and make the blackness a lifestyle is so tragic. While this person was an extreme example, many talented Sagittarian women squander their enormous talents through a self-indulgent tendency to flit through life brilliantly and be a butterfly that never lands.

People can only live up to their creative potential if they focus on where their life is taking them and stop and evaluate their progress. The Sagittarian woman should not cling mindlessly to beliefs that are not serving her well. In doing so she may be making her escape from what she really has to do for herself to be the person her soul needs to be. If her behavior and/or false beliefs are getting in the way of her accomplishments, she needs to really face that—along with the fear. It is necessary to go deeply into herself and dwell there for a while until the truth becomes a fully acknowledged part of her life. What happens most often is that Sagittarius women get distracted and make all kinds of excuses that keep them safely in the same place as time passes and they become increasingly scattered.

The Sagittarius woman has to take the time to slow down for serious introspection. She has to ask herself questions about what she's really doing. She needs to look at her indulgences and escapes and be honest about what and where they are bringing her. All of this takes time. Time and consciousness are her path to wisdom. Wisdom is an old crone who doesn't have to run from fear anymore. She is free through what she has come to know about her life through the depths of her soul. The brilliance of wisdom is the jewel waiting at each stage of the journey's spiral. Whether the spiral goes up into the light or down for a time into the darkness doesn't matter. Honor it and commit to the whole journey.

Your Approach to Love

WHILE, LIKE ALL FIRE SIGNS, SAGITTARIANS FEEL IT'S fun to be in love and couldn't care less about the future, the Sagittarian woman is greatly attached to her freedom. She is a footloose and fancy-free adventurer who lives in the moment. And if she is truly typical of her sign, she won't remember the details of the previous day and maybe even a new lover's last name. Now, there is nothing wrong with her memory. It's just that she has a brain that is taking in so much around her that she often has little time for details. She also has a fast mind and a fleeting attention span that sometimes gets in the way of working at things, especially relationships.

The Sagittarian woman is not one who will ever be found barefoot, pregnant and chained to a bed. Or chained to anyone, as a matter of fact. Everything she does must be her choice. She is a law unto herself. An intense individual in style, ambition and philosophy, she goes about her life fueled by fascinating facts and future plans. And in the scheme of things, marriage is usually not first on her list.

She is so preoccupied with adventure, nature, learning and exploring—both inner and outer terrains—that she would be the last to decide that her life is devoid of meaning if she doesn't have a date—or a "meaningful relationship." The Sagittarian woman is a seeker of meaning in a lot of ways. Like her personality, her interests can't be confined—which often applies to her lovers.

Although she is capable of playing the field and remaining uncommitted, the man most likely to capture her attention would have to be a very bright flame. The Sagittarian woman is bored by limitation. She wants to be at the top of a mountain with the wind in her face and can't bear pulling someone up by the collar. She needs a partner who is a friend and an equal, not an excuse for a connection. Because, as a Sagittarian, she holds so fast to truth and her ideals, she is going to keep moving until she meets him.

There may be times when a woman born under this sign may seem too impatient and insensitive. That is a very real part of her. However, she is also a generous expansive person prepared to offer as much as she hopes to receive—and that's a lot.

She is also forever growing and expanding and trying to better herself. The Sagittarian woman can be a wonder unto herself. However, for the wrong person she's impossible. A man must have a very sturdy ego if he intends to captivate her. For one thing, she has an emotional hearing problem coupled with a plethora of opinions. On her causes and ideals no one can counter her. However, instinctively, the Sagittarian woman understands something terribly important about love: You don't have to give yourself up or throw yourself away to have it. You just have to be yourself for yourself and go halfway.

Sagittarius is a great animal lover who could make a panther purr. She's also a great friend who would give away her last dollar to a down and desperate chum. But whatever she chooses to be, she stands tall in who she is. Most of all, the Sagittarian woman loves her own life—and it shows. She lives her life with spirit. She respects the earth, the laws of nature and her own potential. She knows there is no other way to grow into her life. The Goddess in her breathes honor into that life. Respect it. Respect all the life around you like your own. And never let a day go by when you don't treat it with love.

Your Power Source

THE SAGITTARIAN SPIRIT, AS IT ACTS ITSELF OUT IN THE everyday, is a tonic for those it touches and a force of light for those less inspired. At its best, this expansive lover of life and generous goodwill to others is a doorway for Sagittarians to human greatness.

Sagittarius is associated with the ninth house of the higher mind. It is also the house of higher intellectual learning, religion, philosophy and spiritual seeking. Sagittarian women need to seek in order to satisfy their soul. They need to encounter their own spiritual power in many ways—through increased learning, greater understanding and more conscious loving. They also need to incorporate what they learn into their daily lives so that it becomes a source of meaning that sustains them. The luminous Sagittarian spirit should never be taken for granted. It should be nurtured so that it flourishes enough to cushion its bearer against the spiritual sterility of the tension-ridden world.

There is a faith within the Sagittarian soul that we can all learn from. Sagittarius is commonly associated with good luck. However, what this luck is is the outgrowth of faith. Sagittarian women were born with the power of positive thinking. Because they are an active fire sign, they put it to good use and benefit from its results.

There is a doctrine in Taoist philosophy called "Wu Wei," which loosely means yielding to the flow of an occurrence in such a way that the best overall realization is brought about. For example, don't get terribly upset and resist the disturbance. What seems to be an obstacle might be a significant opportunity that you can't see at the moment. Look for the meaning and the light that will lead you to a better place. This is very much the sort of faith and optimism the Sagittarian woman has. As a mutable sign, she sees that there are many possibilities in any given situation, even if she can't see half of them herself. At a certain point her curiosity and sense of adventure also kick in. This causes her to get caught up in the potential for future gain instead of being buried in the bad fortune of the present. The most wonderful part of this is that such an attitude is infectious. Once you see someone handle themselves in an uplifting manner, you can't help but be inspired yourself.

The Sagittarian woman should use her creativity to spread this wonderful spirit out into the world in all kinds of ways that are fun for her. Simply by example she is a teacher. One method of her teaching is her spontaneous personality and sense of humor. She can laugh at something that would be a dreadful upset to someone else. She can also laugh at herself. Another important way in which she is a powerful teacher is through her love of life. She is a true individual and she values that and the blessed life force within her. It is so easy for women to become influenced by the superficial standards our society sets up for us, standards by which so many women sadly measure their worth. The Sagittarian woman sets her own standards and is so preoccupied with the things in her life she considers meaningful that she is impervious to all the shallow attitudes of advertising. What is important in her life is what she wants to do with it. She dwells in a place of anticipation, not insecurity—anticipation of all the things she wants to do and places she wants to travel to—in her mind, spirit and self. The Sagittarian woman knows that life was meant to be lived and she is impatient to get on with it because she sees it all as an unending discovery destined to take her to fascinating places.

The Sagittarian woman loves to learn. She is never lacking because she is always moving, growing, experimenting and adventuring. Instead of being dependent on people or things on the outside for her well-being, she is a self-generating individual. Her courage and enthusiasm come from inside. On the inside she knows that it's up to her what she creates on the outside.

And she wants to paint the sky with her dreams and ideals.

A Sagittarian knows that her dreams and ideals don't always come to fruition. And that's okay. Despite her plethora of lofty attitudes she accepts that she's just human. Besides, she has such an abundant dream supply that there is never a dearth of new ideas. Broken dreams are only moments. However, there is always another day and another possibility already unfolding on some unseen plane. In the meantime she has something very exciting—she has herself and she has the joy of exploring who she might become. All women who want to escape themselves through anything or anyone outside themselves would benefit by being around a Sagittarian for a while. She knows how to be joyful—on a shoestring, by herself without a man, in the woods talking to wild things, in a large group of crazy people, or in solitude creating. So she gets right past all those petty things that always get in the way and gets on with it—her life!

At her height, the Sagittarius woman's faith in her inner wisdom is a source of brilliant clarity. She is so vibrant in spirit that she can turn mundane acts into prayers through the sacred attention she bestows upon them. She chooses to use this power in a way that helps illuminate the world around her. This is a grace. It is a gift not forgotten in the surrounding swirl of mechanistic madness. Furthermore, she is so willing to share it and convince everyone that they have it too. Her loving generosity profoundly penetrates both the human heart and the animal soul, the only fitting resting places for such divine spirit.

CAPRICORN

(December 22–January 20)

Your Essential Nature

THE EARTH SIGN ASSOCIATED WITH THE MOUNTAINS, Capricorn is concerned with ascent. A climber toward greater material possibility, the Capricorn woman is ambitious and pragmatic, goal oriented and prepared to do whatever it takes to attain her desires. From childhood on, she is often older and more mature than her peers. As an adult, she knows how to put the past and the present to practical, profitable use and she will do this with a grounded focus and relentless energy that usually guarantee success.

A highly organized initiator, she often has a strong impact on the outside world. The Capricorn woman is a leader in business and a potential tycoon in whatever area she decides to take on. Hardworking, tenacious and totally committed to her goals, she is an example of what it takes to be a solid superachiever.

The Capricorn woman builds her empire stone by stone, looking ahead to see the big picture, while keeping in mind all the small essential details. Like her natural element, earth, she is solid and enduring, gravitating toward what is substantial and of worth, creating it and collecting it through a sharp, discriminating headset.

A woman who takes life, herself and her loved ones very seriously, she has no time for trifles. Likewise, she is not to be toyed with. Having a fierce sense of pride and a fear of surprises, she controls her environment through her ironclad expectations that sees to it that everyone and everything has a place and is in it securely.

Highly self-critical and deeply self-conscious, she applies perfectionistic standards to herself that she rigidly tries to live by. Status oriented and strongly fashion conscious, she tries to mold herself to trendsetting standards that satisfy her need for attention and adulation from the world at large. The classic Capricorn woman needs to be out in the world and on top of it, dictating from a lofty perch that she created for herself through striving, natural smarts, know-how and a no-nonsense approach to power.

Elizabeth Arden is the most outstanding example of the kind of Capricorn sense of enterprise that can turn an ambition into a billion-dollar industry. An unmarried young woman in her late twenties living in the boondocks of Canada with her father, she came to New York penniless but proud. Working day and night on a little formula for face cream that she marketed and developed slowly, she eventually expanded to other products as well and sold hundred-dollar handbags during the Depression when one dollar could mean a week's food! Her business became so enterprising that it even eventually included Maine Chance, a highly exclusive health spa which was groundbreaking in this country at that time. Such is the dynamic, forward thinking business genius of the Capricorn mind, a mind that can make big things happen through a bottom line business attitude and goals that reach to the sky.

Yet material success is not the entire picture of the Capricorn person. This is a woman who also needs close, intimate connections in her life that feed her heart and soul. Capricorn love can run deep and is enduring. A faithful mate and forever friend, she is a solid, reliable human being who wants to build toward and contribute to a wonderful, enriching future. In this personal realm she will put forth so much effort and give back fourfold from her heart.

Because she is so serious and sincere, the Capricorn woman has her share of searing hurts from callow, shallow fellows who just can't meet her midway. Despite her cool, defensive facade, hurt for a Capricorn woman is like acid in an open wound. However, the single most successful thing about her is that she doesn't hold on to the pain and let it define her. This is a woman who moves on from life's negativities.

Your Dark Side

CAPRICORN IS RULED BY SATURN, THE PLANET OF DISCIpline, restriction and melancholia. However, Saturn also has another side—wisdom and a deep recognition of the value of darkness, that it can lead to light. Darkness and light are opposite sides of the same coin and that coin can flip over despite the enormous ego power of the Capricorn woman.

The dark side of the Capricorn woman takes the form of depression, moodiness or such rigid self-discipline that it abnegates self-love. This is a woman who judges herself according to the judgments of society at large—standards that are not in a woman's best self-interest to embrace. The Capricorn woman often derives great ego gratification from conforming to and being a perfect example of some of society's most shallow values. Material power, youth, beauty and a perfect body embrace this continuum and can also contribute to great self-loathing if she doesn't measure up. A few extra pounds or a rounded belly simply disgusts her and has to be gotten rid of in record time. Working to attain the peaks of physical perfection gives her a sense of control and power—but this often comes at the cost to her total self.

A Capricorn woman doesn't want to deal with deeper emotions. Even when they keep cropping up, she will try to ignore them with a routine of dynamic activity and exercise. However, at some point in her life, if she is going to become more than a one-dimensional person, the Capricorn woman has to realize that there is more to her and her potential than control and the stuff society's values provide. There is also a soul inside her that must be acknowledged and tended to. It is usually the case that Capricorn women start to experience their soul through love.

Love can and usually does overturn the tidy applecart. All of Capricorn's control tactics have no place to go here and her ego defensiveness is certain to get her exactly what she doesn't want: rejection. Love for the Capricorn woman is often a great initiation into the depths of her being. Often the road is bumpy and involves many learning experiences and some serious disappointments. It is through these trials that the Capricorn woman starts to live more authentically, embracing her feelings and starting to realize the importance of having her emotions, not merely her ego satisfied.

Deep love gives the Capricorn woman a meaning that can make her outward success seem empty by contrast. This is the real challenge of her journey: emotional meaning versus the merely material. In a Capricorn woman's life both are important, both have to be balanced in value if she is going to move past the level of the purely superficial. And, at some point, she has to move past this level if she is to be grounded in herself and if she is to grow through herself.

Therefore, it is important for the Capricorn woman to keep in mind that the disappointments in love and the darkness associated with lack of love are all waking her up to deeper parts of herself. Where there is darkness, there is also light straining to come through. However, this is a process and like all processes, has its own time. In the meantime, the more honest a Capricorn woman can be with herself and the kinder she can be to herself, the more she will start to value the deeper range of herself. And as these deeper levels slowly become more conscious, they will bring her to new worthwhile experiences and people.

As she gets older, the woman born under this sign faces the challenge of treating herself as an individual as opposed to a carbon copy of society's material values. The more that she does this, the less she is operating from a facade or a defense; she is beginning to operate from an authentic place that permits her to feel all kinds of emotions she was never capable of before. She has grown. She is now more of herself and she will find that it is very freeing.

There is no real defense against the darkness in our lives, especially when it rises up from our own souls.

But there is always the power of light, the light of our souls which is the light of meaning and deeper understanding. Her own depths are the Capricorn woman's greatest challenge in life. However, by living through them, instead of running from them, she can find her greatest power.

Your Approach to Love

LOVE IS A CRITICAL FACTOR IN THE CAPRICORN WOMan's life. It is where she encounters her feminine soul. Often, in a lifetime, the issue of relationship turns out to be a cross which Capricorn must bear again and again.

Usually Capricorn's early years are fraught with a good deal of disappointments. These disappointments come from being attracted to the wrong men, or at least, to men who have a lot of their own lessons to learn. At the time the Capricorn woman meets these men they usually sparkle with excitement or have a kind of social or material power that makes them seem highly desirable. They often have a high-profile identity that is impressive in some way. Often the Capricorn women can't see beyond it and their sexual attraction. This sort of man takes his cues from himself, rather than trying to conform to something outside of himself. He is his own reward and everything about him communicates that. The Capricorn woman often has a great deal to learn from this kind of man. He teaches her the power individuality has to make a stamp on society, rather than the other way around, which tends to be the trap of so many women.

When the Capricorn woman is in love, she extends

her boundaries to do a lot of things that she would never think of doing out of love. What she will give and the degree to which she is willing to accommodate takes her beyond herself. Even the hardest of Capricorn career women have been known to do their lover's laundry. However, often Capricorn women suffer at the hands of the sparkly fellows who attract them. For one, these "boys" are very selfish. And two, they often don't value love.

After a number of years of being patient, positive, dynamic, constructive and very giving to these sorts of guys, the Capricorn woman gets fed up. At a certain point she begins to realize that she's putting too much energy out and not getting enough back to sustain her in any meaningful way. At this point, she usually finds the strength to end the relationship.

When something starts to change deep inside of the Capricorn woman and she begins to be conscious of a part of her that really needs a quality connection with real closeness, trust and intimacy, quite magically, a deeper, richer love experience often enters her life. However, this sort of love takes a level of maturity that she didn't have when she was busy seeking excitement. The Capricorn woman is Saturn's child, and Saturn is the planet of the wheel of time. In this aspect, Saturn also points to the richness and power of process, how through process we start to see differently and start to attract different things into our lives.

Through this deeper, richer kind of love the Capricorn woman allows herself to be nourished. She is no longer the one who is waiting, giving, running and scrambling frenetically to hold everything together. Now there are two people who both want to give and who see that that desire is more important than the mere desire of sex. This new relationship doesn't exclude sexual desire, but it includes it in a context that is much vaster, wondrous and full of mystery. Through this mystery the Capricorn woman becomes acquainted with the mystery of herself, her soul, the feminine within her, which is deep and rich and ancient. And once she has come to see it and own it in her own way, this power within will be ever unfolding in her life.

Your Power Source

SO MANY WOMEN STRUGGLE WITH THEIR WORTH. THE Capricorn woman understands her worth in material terms which means being able to put a price on something she has created—whether that be a business venture, her crafts or her services. She can make her ideas concrete and has the self-starting initiative to get them out in the world in the right way.

Capricorn is cardinal earth. Cardinal is the ability to start something in a dynamic way, while earth involves making the undertaking solid and substantial. Capricorn women have a great deal of common sense combined with practical know-how. Consequently, they can make their dreams come true and they can also profit from them. Capricorn women are great idea people who love to create something out of nothing and then watch it build, step by step.

In this sense, Capricorns have a primal creative ability that other women can learn from. Capricorn women can inspire others to follow their visions and can help them understand all the practical steps that go into getting their dreams materialized. They are capable of accomplishing many dreams in one lifetime and of creating many different successful businesses. Instinctively, they understand the necessity of pushing creative urges past the thinking stage and *doing* something about them.

The Capricorn woman's unique gift is that she knows how to get things done—and done right. She takes herself and her creations seriously. She also values herself, her body and her performance.

The Capricorn woman treats her body as a significant vessel that must be tended to, nourished and cared for. She puts time and effort into her health and exercise regimens, just as she puts time and effort into her relationships.

She is a loyal, deeply loving friend, mother, lover and wife. The Capricorn woman is there in a crisis and takes charge. However, she is also there, over the years, in her heart, her memory and her soulful feeling for deep, close personal connections. She is an active participant in her relationships with others, just as she is in her relationship with the world. She can be a powerful fund-raiser for charity causes and an invaluable organizer for volunteer organizations that otherwise could never get off the ground. She can also be powerful in politics, fighting relentlessly for legislation that breaks through outworn boundaries and promotes social progress.

The Capricorn woman is strong, enduring and constant. Responsible, steadfast and having a high set of standards and ethics, she is a forceful, dynamic woman who knows the power of getting what she wants, regardless of frustrations, obstacles and other people's fear. Whatever gets in her way doesn't stay there for long. With her enormous energy the Capricorn woman can break up mountain ranges and then reassemble them to her specifications. Hers is the power of self-actualization and she stands tall in her own power, a power that can improve the world in so many ways. The Capricorn woman is a mover made to make positive use of herself. And she does just that.

AQUARIUS
(January 21–February 19)

Your Essential Self

THE MOST IDEALISTIC OF SIGNS, THE TYPICAL AQUARIUS woman is something of a law unto herself. Ruled by the planet Uranus, which signifies independence, freedom, humanism, and futuristic concepts, it is not easy for her to live comfortably in this world of empty outworn social conventions which can sometimes be very limiting. In her mind, the Aquarius woman is a seeker of truth and a rebel against the grosser forms of human life like greed, cruelty, discrimination and social systems that dehumanize the individual. A champion of the underdog and a do-gooder for the weak and damaged, she looks at the world, not in terms of how it is, but only as it should be.

She can be blind to all ideas but her own and in this way, she can be very unbalanced. When she is unbalanced, she is led away from all the ideas and ideals she wants to accomplish. However, one must bear in mind that the Aquarius woman is an air sign and, like all air signs, she tends to live in her head. The danger of living too much in the head is that one can become divorced from reality. There *is* a world out there and sometimes it differs markedly from the world within. This split between inner and outer realities sometimes happens to the Aquarius woman and when it does, it can get her into some difficulties. For instance, often Aquarians don't see a person or situation for who or what it really is and therefore can become a victim to that person or force. Aquarius has a tough time changing her views. Aquarius's view of a situation or person stays pretty rigid, even if it doesn't at all resemble the reality.

Nevertheless, the Aquarius woman is often brilliant, insightful and bursting with bubbles of great lucidity. She is also often ahead of her time and mentally beyond the social framework that surrounds her. The typical Aquarius is not afraid of challenging the status quo, nor is she overly concerned with being liked. When focused on a mission, she is concerned only with getting it accomplished and has no peripheral vision for the feelings, rules and regulations lined up on either side of her mental course.

She is the first to be attracted to "New Age" ideas. To her, they are obviously old wisdom. She is also intellectually open to all kinds of realities and ways of thinking that might seem silly or flaky to an earth sign. Her mind is like a changing room for all kinds of progressive ideas. In line with this, she is most attracted to other people who stimulate her thinking. She can be interested in so many things and talented in so many areas that she really has to be careful of scattering her energies.

As a person, the Aquarian woman tries to be understanding and giving even if people sometimes take advantage of her. She is the first to respect human suffering and the last to say no to a friend in need. In this sense she can sometimes be a sort of savior to the needy and not a very good friend to herself. This always reminds me of an Aquarius woman I knew who came upon a homeless woman sitting on the subway steps begging for money for food. She ran to the nearest deli and bought a huge roast beef sandwich with potato salad and happily brought it back to her. The woman threw it on the ground, cursed her and screamed that she wanted MONEY!

The Aquarius woman has to be prudent and aware that some people may not value her generous nature. Otherwise, she can give herself away in her idealistic desire to help the wrong people. She also has to become aware that there are different ways to help—a right way and a wrong way. Simply to help blindly can be a wrong way, not only for herself, but also for the other person.

The sun is in its detriment in Aquarius, which means that there is not a good sense of boundaries and self-preservation in this sign. The Aquarian woman can neglect herself as she plunges into the problems of others—who, in fact, might need to learn to stand alone. She has to learn first and foremost that she has a moral responsibility and an ethical obligation to be conscious and to take care of herself—or else she may end up in worse shape than the people she is helping. She has no one to understand that if that happens, she has no one to blame but herself.

Just as Aquarian women like to help victims, they also like to talk as if they were victims. Aquarians often have a complete repertoire of stories about how someone or several people took away their money, their business, their freedom—when all they did was be so kind. Five years later, if you meet the same Aquarian, you hear the same story but the names of the selfish evil characters have changed and there is a new set of sad circumstances. Aquarian women often allow themselves to be victims of their children, who they allow to stomp all over them in workman's boots. Because Aquarian women have no boundaries, their children usually don't either. So the message that they get from Mother is YES, you can take advantage.

The Aquarian woman needs a lot of space. The space factor is about maintaining a situation in which life is open ended and anything interesting can happen at any time. Aquarians feast their minds on what might be, what should be and what could be, regardless. So when they create traps for themselves through being fixed and not adapting to the reality of the situation, it always seems as if these traps were coming at them from the outside. It has nothing to do with their choices. As far as they are concerned, it has nothing to do with other people.

Aquarian women have to find their own way, beyond traps, to the living situation which uniquely suits them. Whatever they do, it has to be in their own way and through their own timing. When someone tries to thwart them or invade their space, Aquarians can be cold, cruel and very defiant. They have to be pushed to this difficult and defensive place before they realize they have boundaries and how important it is to maintain them. An Aquarius woman who allows her boundaries to be trampled and her mental space snuffed out can become sick, very sick. At all times she must be conscious of her own nature and never undermine it for *any* reason. She has a responsibility to herself to be true to herself—and to tell herself the truth. This means recognizing *her* part in the play that she wants her life to become—and consciously acting on it.

Your Dark Side

IDEALISTIC AND CONNECTING THEIR EGO WITH THEIR ideals, most Aquarian women don't want to think about their unconscious dark side. Therefore, they tend to project their shadow onto others. When the Aquarius woman has a problem being controlling, she will quite mysteriously find controlling people in her life who intensely annoy her. Because she tends not to deal with her anger directly, the same thing will happen when confronted with people full of anger issues. Likewise, if she is not conscious about her own dishonesty, she will attract people who lie to her and cheat her. Therefore, it is sufficient to say that when there are repeated, chronic problems with other people around an issue, the Aquarius woman has got to start to do some serious emotional inventory.

Likewise, it is important for the Aquarius woman to own her feelings. This can be a hard one since she is an air sign and air signs can get so caught up in thinking that sometimes they often don't know what they're really feeling. Experience can be processed through the mind so intensely that it comes out the other end as one long thought. That is, air signs tend not to take thoughts and feelings down into their souls and experience them. They'll pass through their mind without ever sinking deeper. And when that happens repeatedly, they get out of touch with the deeper parts of themselves.

When an Aquarius woman is emotionally upset she will tend to talk a great deal. That is great for starters but there is a delicate line where her experience can get forced into a rush of words that float on the air and disappear. If this happens the Aquarian doesn't get deeper into the meaning of the experience. Everything that happens to us has a meaning that says something about us. Therefore, it is important to ask oneself what the message is and how to best benefit from it.

There is always a message. When you understand it, it will be a freeing and empowering experience. The message might be about your boundaries—about being up-front as to what you can and cannot do. Maybe you allowed this person so much latitude that they stepped right into the wrong place, took you for granted and then took you for a ride. Or maybe it's a different message. But if you reflect on the situation long enough, you will understand the meaning of the experience and you will be able to benefit from it.

Sometimes the Aquarius woman has to give herself time for things to filter down so she can really feel them. Of course this can be painful—but it is also necessary. When she can feel, she can act. However, when she pushes everything into thoughts and won't let anyone sink deeper, the experience stays in her consciousness as muck and never gets transformed into insight and wisdom.

Aquarius is a fixed sign and fixed means FIXED—staying in a situation too long. Aquarius is also fixed air which means holding on to a headset that is no longer meaningful in life. As I have said before, this is a sign that can get a divorce and then remain in the same relationship that denied the entire individuality. What is known was in the past and may have been terrible, but it is still secure because it is familiar. This is the negative aspect of the Aquarius woman.

When an Aquarius woman is conscious, values herself and her life and is responsible to herself, then she is armed for change. The problem is that air signs especially want quick fixes and nothing is ever that simple or that easy. The important thing to remember is that if you really want to walk away from your darkness, however it is manifesting in your life, the time to start is now. If you are really committed to bringing about positive change, down to the depths of your soul, you will start to look at your life for its lessons and you will be open to hearing and seeing your own truth as it happens every day. The universe will help you in many ways because your unconscious knows that you have said "yes!" to yourself and to all the possibility that can come from that.

Your Approach to Love

EVERYONE WANTS LOVE TO GRACE THEIR LIVES. YET, for the Aquarius woman this is not an easy area. Living so much of her life in her head, she can get out of touch with her deeper feelings. She also needs a great deal of freedom and space which can conflict with the demands of a conventional relationship.

Suited to the unconventional and to distance producing situations, Aquarius women have been known to happily carry on relationships from afar. Love affairs across states or countries, relationships with married men as well as men in problematic situations who can't commit are all typical for the freedom loving Aquarian woman. What is also common is for her to postpone marriage for years and years and years, or to divorce her husband only to start dating him again. One Aquarius woman I knew divorced her husband and ended up living with him as if he were her brother. In this arrangement, they both saw other people at the same time that they also shared a family lifestyle. One day, her ex-husband introduced her to someone and he stopped, completely stumped at trying to define his relationship to her. It was so confusing to everybody what they were still doing together.

Aquarian relationships can be confusing because this is not a sign that was made for too much closeness. Aquarian women are easily suffocated and need relationships that allow them to express their individuality. A lot of men are threatened by women who are very independent and willful and out of fear and anxiety they try to impose situations and limitations upon them that are stifling. This can create a great conflict for this woman who wants to love but doesn't want to lose herself.

Every Aquarius must find her own solution to this problem. Some Aquarian women who have been burdened by the deadness of an empty marriage decide for a time that they are simply happier alone. Others might find a man who is more of a friend and who isn't around a lot. Others get lucky and manage to find a man who also likes his space and values that in her.

Communication is extremely important to women born under this sign, who, like the Gemini woman, need someone to really talk to. And, like the Gemini woman, the Aquarius woman has to also like the "idea" of the man. Ideally, he will be brilliant, dashing, energetic or simply very, very smart in ways that she can learn from. He must also be something of a challenge, requiring her to stretch. However, should he act clingy and start to breathe down her neck, it won't matter how brilliant or sexy he may be. He is destined to become history.

The Aquarius woman needs a man she respects who is a partner, not a problem to be overcome. Ideally, he is also a friend with whom she shares a strong mental, emotional and sexual rapport. The more she can share as equals with her man, the more she can love and be free in the most challenging way—free to care for someone else deeply *and* be herself, her unique self.

Your Power Source

AT HER MOST POWERFUL, THE AQUARIUS WOMAN LIVES through an affirmative individuality which can be an example to other women. Just as she values her own individuality, she treats the individuality of others with respect. Independent and strong willed, she thinks for herself, holds firm to her convictions and is not afraid to speak out for what she believes in. Often she takes on worthwhile causes for the benefit of others, while on a personal level she has a strong sense of caring and can be counted on for support and a helping hand when needed.

With her outgoing personality and great sense of humor, the Aquarius woman makes a great group leader. Often her mind is ahead of its time and she sees beyond social roles and stereotypes to what is really important. Aquarius is a sign known for its brilliance, its search for personal and universal truth and its desire to make a difference in the world. Of course, this often conflicts with personal desires and concerns, like ongoing love relationships. The Aquarius woman struggles to live up to the potential of her independent nature and at the same time maintain a love relationship that stimulates her and doesn't smother her. This is no easy task.

The late great astrologer Grant Lewis once said that the positive Aquarius moves from fear to faith. I think this is beautifully expressed. To get beyond fear to a faith-based view of one's own future is a powerful position. The positive Aquarius woman faces herself with courage, regardless of her tests, and each time she does so she gains a new strength. As this strength evolves and accrues through the passing years, the Aquarius woman becomes capable of new challenges. She also attracts new people into her life who reflect this positivity. When the Aquarius woman shares her energy with others in ways that are meaningful to her individuality, she is also expanding herself in powerful ways. She is expanding outward and away from the littleness that can consume so many people and trap them in a life that is small, dull, empty and defined by routine.

A great example of an Aquarius woman who is a powerful self-actualizer is Oprah Winfrey. Living out her own path in the world with courage, compassion for others and great emotional integrity, she is a powerful force for communication, activism and social commitment. A woman with a great humanitarian heart who gives out to others and herself in the most constructive ways, she is a role model for women of all ages in this age when so many destructive values reign that diminish women's self-esteem and sense of human potential.

Aquarius women can spiritually revitalize themselves and others through their vision, will and pervasive spirit. The positive Aquarius woman refuses to be trapped and held hostage by anything—a bad marriage, a negative job, an abusive or boring relationship. Against all odds they break free and create new positive change for themselves, inspiring other women to do the same.

While it is true that we cannot change another person, the way we live affects others. At its best, the life force of Aquarius women makes strident statements about the human richness and meaning of living freely and authentically. This means living from who you are uniquely—not from who others expect you to be or tell you you have to be, but *only* who you know you must be for yourself. That doesn't mean that there is always a clear image of this in mind; it means that there is a conscious recognition of the power and integrity of one's own soul. This inner prompting is what becomes the path to awakening.

When Aquarius women work to become conscious about their special place and purpose, they are using their Goddess power. They are treating themselves as sacred and honoring the divine spark within them.

The Aquarius woman who practices this is very concerned with meaning. She knows that the sorrows as well as the joys have a meaning that can lead her somewhere. She may not always understand at the moment; the understanding may take years. However, she does understand that she is meant to know the meaning of her life and will work to discover it.

Hers is the eleventh sign out of the twelve signs of the zodiac. That means she holds the accumulation of lessons and wisdom of all of the previous signs. How to use herself best in a way that will most satisfy her and her changing needs is one of many issues that keep circling around in her brain. Why? Perhaps because there are many answers and many ways. There are so many things an Aquarius woman wants to do and can do. It is her creative task and responsibility to make the best decision for herself.

I remember a very brilliant man once saying, "They think they have all the answers and they don't even know the right questions." Questions—the right questions—are so important because they move you along. The Aquarius woman's mind is fertilized with questions. They start as a child with "Why do I have to do that?" "Do I really have to do that?" resulting in "I don't think I have to do that." And so it goes on through adult life. The nature of the voice changes. The kinds of questions change. Nevertheless, they keep coming. And the answers keep coming. This natural questioning process and the answers that come from it, along with her active kindness toward others, make the Aquarius woman a Goddess of her own making. She is the great author of herself and she makes her life a continual creation.

PISCES

(February 20–March 20)

Your Essential Self

IMAGINATIVE, INTUITIVE AND FEMININE TO THE CORE, the Pisces woman is changeable, fluid and filled with fantasies of how she would like life to be. Not only does she believe in the magic of life, she can conjure it up through a mind that is extraordinarily visual. The Pisces woman believes in possibility and one of her gifts is that she can also create it.

Ruled by Neptune, the planet of mysticism, divine inspiration, escapism and the psychic realm, the Pisces woman can be a mystery unto herself. A shape changer who can turn into very different people at different times, she can be both warm and feeling as well as cool and distant. She can be childlike and impressionable or cynical and instinctively manipulative. She can be wildly enthusiastic or hysterically fearful. She can appear totally *there* only to have disappeared to a secret place inside her head. She can be many things and be in many places in her imagination but one thing she is, above all, is a believer in fairy tales coming true. Most of her life stories contain herself starring as the princess.

The imagination of the Pisces woman is boundless, so boundless that sometimes it interferes with her sense of reality. She loves what is colorful, sparkling and larger than life. Whether that is glamour and fame, seeing herself cast in a grand life role or feeling she is intimately participating in the mystical mysteries of the universe, she needs to embrace an expansive, open-ended view of life.

In this way, she can be truly inspiring because she has an uncanny way of focusing her mind and emotions on a goal and making it happen. Pisces has a great natural ability to visualize. Her mind can easily drift off into daydreams that start to seem real and she can imagine all the vivid details in such a way that they start to take over her life and become concrete goals. She has a strong, instinctive sense of theater which she invests in any pursuit truly important to her. So, whether she is discussing her spirituality, the love of her life or her dreams and ambitions for her future, she makes the telling so emotionally vivid that it seems cinematic.

She will not be bored by the banal, colorless or mundane. Likewise, she won't dull her creative mind with too many long drawn out details. A grand intuitive, she is quick to get the big picture which is all that happens to interest her. Other people can organize and analyze all they want, what she finds important is her feeling and imagination.

Not only does she believe in magic, she relies on it. She "knows" that there are "on" days and "void" days and it is important to treat them according to their nature. She is also aware of signs or metaphors in her environment that are messages from the universe. She knows that everything that does happen has a reason and a meaning. Nothing is arbitrary. The universe is a vast unfolding of untold mysteries and she has her own unique place in it.

Although their intuitions are often uncannily correct, Pisces women can be emotionally subjective. Here, they can be vulnerable to manipulation around things they want to believe in. So, anyone who supports them in their vision and better yet, provides a new source of sparkle, will have enormous influence in their lives—for good or ill.

Pisces women are true romantics in every sense of the word. They want castles and heroes, not politically correct men with no pizzazz. They gravitate toward stars, spiritual masters and anyone with a title, a manor house and a lot of larger-than-life privileges. Yes, they are influenced by razzle-dazzle on the outside. Sometimes they are blinded by it. Like a moth to a flame, Piscean women often fly toward power in its many forms. When they find it, they feel part of it. Pisces women psychologically merge with that with which they want to identify. It might be the most successful aspect of their sense of whimsy to want what they feel they deserve, whether or not that is realistic. Pisces women are never confused by the facts. They live freely in their imagination. And wherever that takes them, that's where they'll reside—for a while.

Your Dark Side

THE DARK SIDE OF ALL OF THE WATER SIGNS IS BASED on fear—the kind of fear that comes not from real life threats so much as from the imagination. Water signs can easily imagine all the possibilities in a situation, including the worst outcome. Of the three water signs, Pisces is the most imaginative.

Pisces is also psychically sensitive and lives close to the unconscious, with floods of thoughts and images surfacing from time to time. There are so many flurries of moods and thoughts that pass through the Pisces mind that they become fluctuations that are easily forgettable. Pisces is a changeable sign, not so much from will, but from feeling. It is also an intuitive, receptive sign, a psychic sponge of sorts that sometimes picks up the negativity of other people without even realizing it.

Like a stream of water in nature, Piscean emotions have to flow. They need the right outlets or else they can become like a murky, slimy pond. Because Pisces is such a creative and intuitive sign, creativity is not just a wonderful outlet, it is often a necessary one.

The Pisces woman can get so caught up in the experience of others that she loses herself. One end of this spectrum is emotional obsession. Prone to falling in love with problematic men, she can waste her energies on fantasies that insidiously take over her waking life. Another way a Pisces woman can use herself improperly is through martyrdom, such as sticking by an alcoholic husband or staying in an abusive marriage. This is a sign that can be manipulated through guilt. In a troubled emotional connection, Pisces has a sense that she can or should make it right. The weight is on her shoulders. She carries the pain of the situation like a cross. And usually the pain is from someone else not facing up to themselves.

The ancients called Pisces the sign of sorrow from

self-undoing. Martyrdom, emotional obsession and escapism through addictive behavior undoes the self. In the extreme, through these experiences, there is no sense of self because it has become so fractured and fragmented by forces around it that the consciousness is a blur of psychic and surface impressions.

Pisces women are very impressionable and can be easily influenced by what immediately appeals to them. Likewise, they can be too quick in constructing a numinous meaning to justify their involvement with someone or something that is not right for them. This is part of their need for magic—and the truth is that sometimes they are right. Their intuitions are telling them something important. However, there is a delicate line between this and creative rationalization. For her own safety and well-being the Pisces woman needs to be more analytical and discriminating. She has to work on developing boundaries so that she is not sucked in and swallowed up by negative situations or people. Otherwise, she is contributing to the deadness, destruction and chaos through her own unconscious participation in it.

I was once acquainted with a Pisces woman who suffered her whole life married to a man who was an alcoholic. Her son was also an alcoholic and violent. Her daughter eventually became a drug addict. This woman got through life daydreaming that one day she would escape and go live in the country with her sisters—something she should have done. However, what she did, in fact, was simply be a long-suffering soul who never went anywhere except through her guilt ridden fantasies. One day her son, blindly drunk, decided that he was going to kill his girlfriend. He went to her apartment, broke through the door, grabbed her by the hair, beat her up and strangled her. A neighbor heard her screams and saved her. Valuing her life, the girlfriend got a restraining order and protected herself from any further contact with this woman's son. The woman called her up trying to instigate a reconciliation because her son was "suffering" and she felt so badly. This woman was no martyr. She played her own part in the rampant dysfunction that surrounded her—and it was a very strong, enabling role.

Susceptibility to suffering can be a Pisces woman's downfall. She must understand that she cannot take away another's suffering by denying and negating the joy and possibility in her own life. Indeed, this kind of behavior will increase the darkness. Therefore, Pisces must be very careful of not only who she is saving but "what" she is saving—because the poison can insidiously sabotage her own life.

Your Approach to Love

THE PISCES WOMAN APPROACHES ALL OF LIFE THROUGH her feelings. Therefore, whoever is going to get her attention in the area of love, has to appeal to that subjective part of her.

The Pisces woman can be unpredictable. She can also be very changeable and a little quirky. Therefore, a man who may appeal to her at first sight, can turn her off on the next meeting, simply because she doesn't like his choice in shoes. If she dislikes his shoes intensely, she'll start to dislike him too. In a flash, he is no longer luminous. He's become a loser of sorts and it is an opinion that there is no talking her out of. It doesn't matter that she's being irrational and maybe very unfair. These are her feelings in the matter and that's all there is to it.

Whatever is a good word to apply to this woman. She can swim in either direction and blow from hot to cold in record time. There is no predicting the temperature of the weather. It's part of her mystery and it can make her a fascinating person to watch over time.

When someone appeals to the Pisces woman, they have to have mystery, sparkle or a certain power that captivates her attention span. She cannot be captivated by some average guy who tries too hard, or someone so visibly insecure that she has to do all the work. Her need for drama and magic must be met or else her eyes will lose their focus and she will flee.

A favorite Pisces activity is to be so entranced by someone that they forget what time it is, even if hours have passed. They want to feel so magically drawn to a person that they have a sense of two souls merging. To become so totally enchanted that she slips off into a fourth dimension is the sort of phantasmagoria the Pisces woman is basically looking for.

Neptune, the planet that rules Pisces, signifies illusion. It also indicates longing and often Pisces women are more in love with longing than with a real man. Sometimes they only see the persona, the mask that is shown to the world and they miss all the complexities under the surface that make up the person.

Pisces women need fairy tales and fated, sometimes "ill-starred," romances along with a good, healthy dose of glamour and mystery to get their minds churning. That is why they are most suited for Pisces men who are similar and therefore easily provide all these little elements. Two Pisceans are able to create their own little world apart from the rest of the world.

I remember a Pisces woman I once met who spoke to me of her brilliant, mastermind husband who was off in some godforsaken part of the world trying to pull off one of his "great ideas." Often his great ideas wreaked havoc with their finances which would drive an earthbound woman crazy. Of course, an earthbound woman probably wouldn't even listen to his hare-brained schemes in the first place. However, this Pisces woman was very much along for the ride. Her eyes glowed as she said to me, "One thing we're never short of is dreams."

Dreams are the psychic plasma of a Pisces woman. For a man to appeal to the best in her, he has to also appeal to her imagination. And for captivating her imagination and transporting her away from the colorless, banal and mundane, she will share a bit of her soul.

There are dangers the Pisces woman can rush into in her pursuit of great love. One is projecting her self onto a man, making him into a larger than life image and then losing herself to that. When this happens it can be very powerful. The more powerful this transference is, the more she is really encountering herself in him, especially parts of herself that she is not using in conscious creative ways. An example of this is if she falls madly in love with an elusive writer or photographer when those talents are sitting there ripe and waiting to be used in her own unconscious. However, they are not being owned. They are being projected onto someone else—the love object who is using them. This is a common problem in women in general. However, Pisces women have such a need to inflate their objects of desire—sometimes they do it at the cost of themselves. They have to be careful that they are not living out a very creative fantasy and setting themselves up to become obsessed and disillusioned.

Another classic Pisces trap is turning a loser around who has lots of potential. When that sentimental side of her is aroused, she can be pulled around by feelings that it might be best to snuff. Experience will teach anyone who has tried to do this that it is not only impossible, it can also be dangerous when one becomes enslaved in the role of savior.

For a highly imaginative dreamer to live happily in this hard cold world can be challenging. Again and again, one is thrown back on one's illusions. These have to be sorted out from the dreams that can come alive—no easy prospect. However, the most important thing is that the Pisces woman can make her dreams come alive. She has the ability to conjure up in reality the kind of life that suits her.

The Pisces woman is like a poem in search of the writing. What she needs most is another poem who can share her dreams and ideals and maybe even spark some new ones. I think that the Pisces woman is around to show us that dreams are serious business. After all, they can become our life.

Your Power Source

THROUGH THEIR MINDS AND TECHNICOLOR IMAGINATIONS, Pisces women can create miracles and a lot of magic. The visionary aspect of this sign cannot be stressed too strongly. There is an ability to see beyond present limitations or difficulties to another positive possibility that can be so real in her mind that it actually comes true. Many books have been written about the power of visualization. Pisces never had to read a book; they were born knowing its strengths and how to do it.

One of the most wonderful things about Pisces women is that they can be filled with wonder. They can be like children around the Christmas tree. They believe in the sparkly magic inherent in life. And when you're around them long enough, you start to believe it too. I think of a Pisces woman I met recently who told me she was lucky. Things just always came to her. Of course, she expected all kinds of wonderful things to come to her. I said to her that I was sure that this happened because of her attitude. I mentioned a friend I had who was always expecting the worst and I added that, of course, she had had significant tragedy in her life. "Oh," said the Pisces woman, "I've had real tragedy and loss too. But this magical thing keeps happening where wonderful things come to me too. I really think I'm just lucky."

When you think of yourself as lucky, you, of course, become lucky. And it is one powerful attitude. The creative imagination of this sign is boundless. It extends from the arts to real life. When Pisces women use their creativity they are honoring their sacred power and are thereby extending themselves in "magical" directions. They are living through the Goddess within them.

Pisces women can be brilliantly intuitive, emotionally wise and able to enter into the suffering of another and end their isolation in it. Of course, the danger here is that they can also lose themselves to it. Pisces women have to erect strong psychological boundaries. However, once they are up and maintained, Pisces women can make wonderful healers—of the mind, body and spirit.

This is a very spiritual sign. Spiritual involvements have a very expansive effect on the whole psyche. There is so much good that Pisces women can do in the world. One can see the enormous work that Piscean Elizabeth Taylor has done for the AIDS cause even in the midst of her own painful and persistent health problems. When Pisces women direct their sensitivity and compassion to the right outlet, their ability to help others can be pervasive.

However, first they must live through themselves and not try to escape themselves through destructive people or situations. Pisces women have to consciously care for themselves. They must work from the strength in themselves if they are to possess their true power and benefit from it unfolding in their lives. At all times they must take care that they are a full vessel, not an empty one that has been drained of its energies and best intentions. From this place, they have great power to inspire others and bring new life into a barren land.

There is a bit of heaven and all its secrets in the Pisces soul. The powerful Pisces woman knows that, honors it and treats the experience of living as something sacred that will always bring new wonder and wonderful surprises.

EVOKING YOUR GODDESS POWER

Finding the Sacred in the Everyday

THE SECRET TO HAVING THE SACRED IN YOUR EVERY-day is that you have to be willing to find it. This means you have to think about it, you have to generate it and you have to be able to receive it. You have to open yourself to the sacred and you have to keep kindling your relationship with it.

A while ago, I had the unique opportunity to meet, for the first time, a cousin who is a Trappist monk and who has been a hermit in the desolate mountains of Norway for most of his life. He was truly the happiest person I had ever seen in my life. He was so alive and afraid of nothing, having total faith in the power of God. In essence, he was pure, radiant, childlike joy. In talking with him at length, I realized that this wasn't simply mystical magic at work. It was work. Every day he renewed his relationship to God. It was not something he accomplished and took for granted. His life was a living meditation that was a continual process, his every day was a day of prayer that focused his mind and helped him celebrate the divine within him. In an interview with him that I read later he said something that further struck me, "I am afraid that many young people get caught up by the music and the emotional aspect. They think the feelings are love and faith. One day the feelings disappear and with that they think they have also lost their faith. In truth, we must will to believe."

The will is the key to creating the kind of consciousness that invites joy, wisdom and possibility in all things. It is work. We have to remind ourselves and give our souls care just as we give our bodies care.

There are many ways to pray. It can be a matter of talking to a stream, the trees in the forest or the sky, talking from the soul that is, opening the soul up to all the beauty and grace of life. But first, you have to quiet your mind so that it will hear the soul's profound voice. In a busy life you must create a time and a space for yourself that is sacred. Very early in the morning or very late at night are excellent times to do this. Reading something that is soulful and inspiring will help you make the transition from the distracting outer world to the domain of the inner world. Do this every day. Then make up your own prayers. Prayer cleanses the mind. It also helps you to focus on what is important and it will bring to your conscious mind new insights when you are confused. Most of all, prayer connects us to that higher affirmative part of ourselves that has all the power and wisdom that we will ever need.

Get in the habit every day of creating your own soul space. In the background you might want to use some relaxing New Age music. Then maybe you might want to light candles. Look into the flame and create an intimate silence that allows you to feel a deep sense of peace. Talk to the Goddess within you. Ask the Goddess questions and allow yourself to hear the answers. Keep a journal. Decorate the cover with a symbol that is personally significant to you. In the journal, write down what you hear as well as what you especially want to know. Let this book represent the glories and mysteries of your inner domain. Just holding it in your hand will make that domain more concrete for you.

Every day do at least one wonderful thing to pay homage to the creative feminine power within you. Buy a beautiful flower as an offering to your own divinity. Talk to the flower. Flowers are the gifts of the Goddess and they come from blossoms just as you can blossom. Ask the flower how you can flower. Working through images—concrete or purely imagined—is the most powerful way to the jewels of your unconscious.

Every day look for the metaphor in life. Life is always synchronistic. It is always telling us something, but most of the time we are too dull and numb to see and hear and make the kind of brilliant connections that make the experience of life luminous. Be open to the Goddess and listen to her speaking to you. Be able to perceive the messages around you. There are signs and symbols cropping up in life all the time that make life a creative adventure. Sometimes there are warnings. Sometimes there are lessons. Sometimes there are answered prayers. One woman I know says that she has become aware that whenever she is having car trouble it is a signal that she, herself, is off course. If you go through a period when you keep repeatedly losing your glasses, there is often a condition in your life that is begging to be looked at. And, of course, sometimes in the course of a day, a perfect stranger will say something that you need to hear at that point in your life. Stay open and ready to hear and see all the wondrous things you will receive.

Create your own personal bible. Buy a beautiful journal that strongly appeals to you. In that journal record all the quotes from your reading that speak to you inspirationally. On days when you're down, flat, depressed, anxious or uninspired, go to your bible and let it uplift you. It's a good idea to read your favorite quotes every day so that they sift down into the unconscious and become a part of you.

Be conscious of how you treat your mind and where you put it. It is completely deadening to spend too much time watching television or videos. Read inspirational books and great literature that touches your soul. (I have provided a list of wonderful reading at the back of the book to start you off.) Remember that Goddess power is about transporting ourselves. No one can do it for us. It is power that is ours that we have to claim. The power comes in taking active responsibility for our own souls. Wonderful books change the inner landscape. They give you new perspectives. They can completely change the climate of your thoughts. Poetry, literature and spiritual/ psychological books are absolutely essential. They bring range and possibility. Put them in your life and take out the mental garbage. Remember that whatever you feed your mind is part of who you become.

Put good music in your life. Music influences the atmosphere of your mind. The sounds you take in affect your entire nervous system. Start your day with uplifting music that makes you feel more alive. The Baroque composers—Bach, Vivaldi, Telemann, Boccherini, Scarlatti—all heighten the feeling of inspirational joy in life. Their music, composed originally for the church, is completely inspiring. Certain New Age music is good for quieting the mind for contemplation, meditation or creative work. Steven Halpern composes his music scientifically, with the intention of putting the mind in an alpha state. His music is not only relaxing but centering. The music of Haydn and Mozart is also wonderful for creativity of all kinds, while the music of the great medieval mystic, Hildegarde Von Bingen, can really thrust you into the mysterious divine realm of the Goddess. On a very stressed-out day or at a time when you are very angry, anxious or popping out of yourself, put on Chopin's Nocturnes and dance.

Play. Get in touch with your creativity in all kinds of ways. Buy crayons and watercolors and/or acrylics along with a lot of paper. By yourself or with friends, sit down and be a child. Don't think about anything except having fun. See what comes through you. A completely enchanting and exceptionally fun book for a rainy day is *Watercolor for the Artistically Undiscovered,* by Thacher Hurd and John Cassidy (Klutz Press, Palo Alto, California). This is an incredibly imaginative and colorful workbook for adults that is basic and unintimidating. The authors are children's book illustrators and they show you how to create all kinds of flowers and little critters from your own little colorful blobs of paint. This book is all about brush play. Give it to yourself as a nonbirthday gift because you're so special and deserving.

Read fairy tales. Up until the seventeenth century

fairy tales were read by adults, not children. They were relegated to children's fare with the rejection of the irrational that came about in that age. Fairy tales bring us into the magical realm of the imagination and put us in touch with unconscious archtypes in our own psyches. They are also great fun and fabulous ways to stimulate your imagination. Fairy tales evoke the primal creative parts of ourselves that get buried under the stresses and strains of the mundane world. After reading a lot of them, you might even want to write your own and create your own enchanted forest, magic castle and, of course, handsome heroic prince.

Another way to get in touch with the deep inner domain of the Great Goddess is to record your dreams. Of course you're probably not going to remember your dreams every single morning. However, you will remember a lot of them if you really try. Dreams tell us what is happening in our unconscious mind. Our conscious, ego centered mind is really only a small part of us, although that is all that we know. The images in dreams are giving us important messages. And many dreams in a long sequence tell a story about ourselves, our challenges and our future. The unconscious always tells us what we need to know. However, most of the time we are deaf, dumb and blind to it. It also provides a balance for our conscious actions. If we are going too far in one direction and becoming self-destructive, our dreams will warn us. On a less psychological and more purely creative level, dream imagery can be used for poems and the dreams themselves can be used as a muse for fiction writing. Working with dreams in all kinds of ways is a very rich experience that can truly bring you to fascinating places.

Express yourself in writing. Try poetry, fiction, non-fiction, essays or memoirs. It is all wonderful. Have as the aim in your writing the goal of getting into deeper parts of yourself. To do this maybe you're going to have to look at some things in your life in new ways. Maybe you're also going to have to deal with old feelings that have never found a successful expression. Silence the inner critic and have fun.

Keep a journal. On a daily basis write down everything that is important about the day and every day there will be at least one thing that is important on a literal or symbolic level. Reading back over your journal will give you insights into feelings and states of mind that are important but that are completely forgotten by the conscious mind. You can also use your journal to dialogue with yourself. When confused or troubled, ask the two-thousand-year-old Goddess inside of you for meaning and direction. Write the questions in your journal. At some time or another those answers will come.

Create your own mandalas. Mandalas are circles that you decorate any way you want. Dr. Judith Cornell writes in her wonderful book *Mandala* (Quest Books), which I highly recommend, that a mandala that we create "has the regenerative and curative power to activate the latent powers of the mind. . . . It can bring joy as it facilitates the healing of a sense of psychological fragmentation (and) it can give form and expression to an intuitive insight into spiritual truth by releasing the inner light of the soul." This is an extraordinarily beautiful, insightful, fascinating and fun book that will take you on a journey through yourself. She documents how our own mandalas can transform and heal us.

Maintain a relationship with nature. Nature is the domain of the great Goddess. Be in contact with nature as much as possible. If you live in the city, that means walks in the park or getting out of the city on weekends. Go into the woods, sit by a stream, go to the ocean and let your soul come through and speak to you. If you live in the country or suburbs, create a garden. Gardening is very spiritual. It is about respecting and nurturing life. Nature puts us in touch with what's really important.

Become conscious of the cycles of your life and their meaning. As women, we are, in a sense, all lunar creatures, the moon being the great symbol of the feminine principle. We are all aware of the cycles of our bodies. However, we go through cycles with our own psyches as well. There will be a new moon phase, a full moon phase, a dark of the moon phase. It is part of the mystery of being a woman. And each of us has our own unique mystery to live through and our own unique moonbeam path to walk. As you walk along, be conscious of who you are walking with. The wrong people will create an undertow, like the ocean pulling you under. It might be an undertow that takes years to recover from, so you have to be careful. You have to honor yourself and treat yourself as sacred. And therefore, you can only afford to have people around who really treat you with love. Love is the great power of the Goddess, and it all starts with ourselves. Honor the great Goddess within you, and every single day give love to your life and all the possibility within you for more life. Live that love and share it. Bring the sacred to your every day.

The woman who is virgin, one-in-herself, does what she does—not because of any desire to please, not to be liked, or to be approved, even by herself; not because of any desire to gain power over another, to catch his interest or love but because what she does is true.
                    —*Esther Harding,* Woman's Mysteries

CONCLUSION

GODDESS POWER IS ABOUT BECOMING CONSCIOUS OF yourself as an individual female soul. It is about claiming your soul, exploring your soul and valuing the world that is within you. It is about nurturing it, blessing it and encouraging it to unfold to your conscious mind in its own unique way. It is about treating your own soul as sacred, dialoguing with it, feeding it, being creative with it, being open to it—and most of all, not giving it away to something or someone outside yourself that denies it.

When you start to realize that life is not arbitrary, that everything has a meaning that is symbolic of your own process and you start to question what the meaning of occurrences are for you alone, you start to live on another level that is increasingly rich in content and meaning. You are starting to honor your own mystery. You are starting to treat your life as a sacred unfolding. From that sacredness will come more life, creativity and meaning. That doesn't mean that you won't have your bad days, disappointments, perhaps depressions. However, you will become increasingly aware that all of these experiences have a special meaning in your life. They are telling you something and if you can work on hearing it, you will eventually be rewarded with insights that open up your life to a very different kind of experience than it would be otherwise. From this perspective, life is never boring. Every day is different and has something to say to you. There is no end to this creative power—which you can make use of in as many ways as you can possibly think up. Life is increasingly more alive now. It is not just a tangle of meaningless, repetitive outside obligations. Now it is lived around the Source inside of you, the Source of your unique mystery and power. Respect that Source. Talk to it, listen to it, paint it, dance to it. Write down its messages as they come through you. This is your power. This is your divinity. Live it and love it!

One final thought to leave you with. The following is a very beautiful quote that is immensely powerful. Spend some time every week in finding your own quotes that say to you what needs to be said.

Be patient toward all that is unsolved in your heart and ... try to love the questions themselves like locked rooms and like books that are written in a very foreign tongue. Do not now seek the answers, which cannot be given you because you would not be able to live them. And the point is to live everything. Live the questions now. Perhaps you will then gradually, without noticing it, live along some distant day into the answer.

—*Rilke,* Letters to a Young Poet

SUGGESTED READING

Here are some wonderful books to take you farther along on the path to your higher self. To make
this list most accessible, I have broken the books down
into categories of interest. Give yourself the gift of
exploring them.

Creativity Enhancers

Cameron, Julia. *The Artist's Way.* New York: Jeremy P. Tarcher/Perigree Books, 1992.

Cassidy, John and Hurd, Thacher. *Watercolor for
the Artistically Undiscovered.* Palo Alto, California:
Klutz Press, 1992.

Cornell, Judith. *Mandala.* Wheaton, Illinois: Quest
Books, 1994.

Franck, Frederick. *Zen Seeing, Zen Drawing.* New
York: Bantam Books, 1993.

Goldberg, Natalie. *Wild Mind.* New York: Bantam Books, 1990.

Goldberg, Natalie. *Writing Down the Bones.* Boston: Shambala Books, 1986.

Metzger, Deena. *Writing for Your Life.* New York: Harper Collins, 1992.

Nachmanovitch, Stephen. *Free Play.* New York: Jeremy Tarcher/Perigree Books, 1990.

Snow, Kimberly. *Writing Yourself Home.* Emeryville, California: Conari Press, 1989.

Poetry

Barnstone, Aliki and Barnstone, Willis, eds. *A Book of Women Poets From Antiquity to Now.* New York: Schocken Books, 1992.

Dickinson, Emily. *The Complete Poems.* Thomas H. Johnson, ed. Boston: Little, Brown, 1960.

Erdrich, Louise. *Baptism of Desire.* New York: Harper Perennial, 1991.

Halpern, Daniel, ed. *Holy Fire.* New York: Harper Perennial, 1994.

Hirshfield, Jane, ed. *Women in Praise of the Sacred.* New York: Harper Collins, 1994.

Mitchell, Stephen, ed. *The Enlightened Heart.* New York: Harper and Row, 1989.

Oliver, Mary. *House of Light.* Boston: Beacon Press, 1990.

Oliver, Mary. *New and Selected Poems.* Boston: Beacon Press, 1992.

Rilke, Rainer Maria. *Selected Poems.* Translated by Robert Bly. New York: Harper and Row, 1981.

Essays

Rilke, Rainer Maria. *Letters to a Young Poet.* Translated by Stephen Mitchell. New York: Random House, 1984.

Sarton, May. *The House by the Sea.* New York: W. W. Norton & Co., 1977.

Williams, Tempest Terry. *An Unspoken Hunger.* New York: Pantheon Books, 1994.

Reflections on Soul in the Everyday

Moore, Thomas. *Care of the Soul.* New York: Harper Collins, 1992.

Sardello, Robert. *Facing the World with Soul.* Hudson, New York: Lindisfarne Press, 1992.

Welwood, John, ed. *Ordinary Magic.* Boston: Shambala Books, 1992.

Zukav, Gary. *The Seat of the Soul.* New York: Fireside Books, 1990.

Spiritual Enlightenment

Bartholomew. *Reflections of an Elder Brother.* Taos, New Mexico: High Mesa Press, 1989.

Emmanuel. *Emmanuel's Book.* Compiled by Pat Rodegast and Judith Stanton. New York: Bantam Books, 1987.

Emmanuel. *Emmanuel's Book II.* Compiled by Pat Rodegast and Judith Stanton. New York: Bantam Books, 1989.

Roman, Sanaya. *Living With Joy*. Tiburon, California: H. J. Kramer Inc., 1986.

Roman, Sanaya. *Spiritual Growth*. Tiburon, California: H. J. Kramer Inc., 1989.

Feminine Psychology

Anderson, Sherry Ruth and Hopkins, Patricia. *The Feminine Face of God*. New York: Bantam Books, 1991.

Bolen, Jean, M.D. *Goddesses in Every Woman*. New York: Harper and Row, 1984.

Claremont de Castillejo, Irene. *Knowing Woman*. New York: Harper Colophon Books, 1974.

Estes, Clarissa Pinkola. *Women Who Run With the Wolves*. New York: Ballentine Books, 1992.

Harding, Esther. *The Way of All Women*. New York: Harper Colophon Books, 1975.

Harding, Esther. *Woman's Mysteries*. New York: C. J. Jung Foundation, 1971.

Johnson, Robert A. *She*. New York: Perennial Library, 1977.

Luke, Helen. *Woman, Earth and Spirit*. New York: Crossroad, 1993.

Murdock, Maureen. *The Heroine's Journey*. Boston: Shambala, 1990.

Neumann, Eric. *The Fear of the Feminine*. Princeton, New Jersey: Princeton University Press, 1994.

Neumann, Eric. *The Great Mother*. Bollingen Series, Princeton, New Jersey: Princeton University Press, 1963.

Perea, Sylvia Brinton. *Descent to the Goddess.* Toronto, Canada: Inner City Books, 1981.

Toor, Djohariah. *The Road by the River.* New York: St. Martin's Press, 1987.

Von Franz, Marie. *The Feminine in Fairy Tales.* Zurich, Switzerland: Spring Publications, 1972.

Woodman, Marion. *Addiction to Perfection.* Toronto, Canada: Inner City Books, 1982.

Woodman, Marion. *Conscious Femininity.* Toronto, Canada: Inner City Books, 1993.

Woodman, Marion. *Leaving My Father's House.* Toronto, Canada: Inner City Books, 1992.

Woodman, Marion. *The Pregnant Virgin.* Toronto, Canada: Inner City Books, 1985.

Woodman, Marion. *The Ravaged Bridegroom.* Toronto, Canada: Inner City Books, 1990.

About the Author

An astrologer and a writer for over twenty years, Robin MacNaughton is the former astrology columnist for *Harper's Baazar* and author of eleven books, including *Robin MacNaughton's Sun Sign Personality Guide* and *Power Astrology*. She lives in Connecticut.